NEW DIRECTIONS FOR STUDENT SERVICES

Margaret J. Barr, *Northwestern University*
EDITOR-IN-CHIEF

M. Lee Upcraft, *The Pennsylvania State University*
ASSOCIATE EDITOR

Responding to Disability Issues in Student Affairs

Sue Kroeger
University of Minnesota

Judy Schuck
Minneapolis Community College

EDITORS

Number 64, Winter 1993

JOSSEY-BASS PUBLISHERS
San Francisco

CONTENTS

1. Beyond Ramps: New Ways of Viewing Access   5
Jane Jarrow
To understand the current state of disability and higher education, we must
first review the issues and challenges faced over the past two decades.

2. Students' Rights and Responsibilities   17
Salome M. Heyward
The key to compliance with disability discrimination laws is balancing the
rights of disabled individuals with the institution's desire to preserve the
integrity of its programs.

3. Transition to Higher Education   31
Rhona C. Hartman
The period between the end of high school and the beginning of college is
dynamic for any student. Postsecondary institutions need to consider an
array of opportunities as they develop transition programs for undergraduate students of traditional age with disabilities.

4. Creating Positive Outcomes for Students with Disabilities   45
Kevin J. Nutter, Larry J. Ringgenberg
By capitalizing on the strengths of our past and being open to innovation,
student affairs staff can create environments that invite, involve, and retain
students with disabilities.

5. Essential Elements in Effective Service Delivery   59
Judy Schuck, Sue Kroeger
Service delivery systems face many challenges in the 1990s. Coordinating
key features common to successful programs and building in consistent
evaluative practices will enable higher education to achieve full participation by people with disabilities.

6. Students with Learning Disabilities   69
Lydia S. Block
Postsecondary education has become an option for increasing numbers of
individuals with learning disabilities. College personnel must be prepared
to provide academic adjustments and accommodations for the members of
this growing population.

RESPONDING TO DISABILITY ISSUES IN STUDENT AFFAIRS
Sue Kroeger, Judy Schuck (eds.)
New Directions for Student Services, no. 64
Margaret J. Barr, Editor-in-Chief
M. Lee Upcraft, Associate Editor

Microfilm copies of issues and articles are available in 16mm and 35mm, as well as microfiche in 105mm, through University Microfilms Inc., 300 North Zeeb Road, Ann Arbor, Michigan 48106-1346.

LC 85-644751   ISSN 0164-7970   ISBN 1-55542-681-6

NEW DIRECTIONS FOR STUDENT SERVICES is part of The Jossey-Bass Higher and Adult Education Series and is published quarterly by Jossey-Bass Inc., Publishers, 350 Sansome Street, San Francisco, California 94104-1342. Second-class postage paid at San Francisco, California, and at additional mailing offices. POSTMASTER: Send address changes to New Directions for Student Services, Jossey-Bass Inc., Publishers, 350 Sansome Street, San Francisco, California 94104-1342.

SUBSCRIPTIONS for 1993 cost $47.00 for individuals and $62.00 for institutions, agencies, and libraries.

EDITORIAL CORRESPONDENCE should be sent to the Editor-in-Chief, Margaret J. Barr, 633 Clark Street, 2-219, Evanston, Illinois 60208-1103.

Cover photograph by Wernher Krutein/PHOTOVAULT © 1990.

Manufactured in the United States of America. Nearly all Jossey-Bass books, jackets, and periodicals are printed on recycled paper that contains at least 50 percent recycled waste, including 10 percent postconsumer waste. Many of our materials are also printed with vegetable-based inks; during the printing process, these inks emit fewer volatile organic compounds (VOCs) than petroleum-based inks. VOCs contribute to the formation of smog.

EDITORS' NOTES

The world that people have constructed is made by and for nondisabled people—for those who can climb stairs, turn doorknobs and faucets, see where they are going, hear noises and voices, commit instructions and information quickly to memory. Educational programs reflect the values of the world.
—adapted from U.S. Department of Education, *Access for Handicapped Students to Higher Education: A Reference Handbook*, 1981

Few issues on the current agenda of higher education have as much promise for significant change as the policies and practices affecting disabled college students. Emerging from a past that usually regarded disability either as a depressing topic to be avoided or as a minor aspect of other policy issues, this issue now gives college and university administrators and staff an opportunity to acquire a new understanding of the subject and remove crucial barriers that disabled students confront.

Interest in the development of alternative approaches to the analysis of disability has grown in recent years. Much of this growth can be attributed to a significant shift in the definition of disability from the medical orientation, which focuses on functional impairments, and the economic orientation, which concentrates on vocational limitations, to a new, interactional perspective that regards disability as a product of the interaction between the disabled individual and the environment. This paradigm shift is successfully challenging the definitions that have dominated past research and service on disability.

The purpose of this *New Directions for Student Services* volume is to reorient thinking about disabled students. Seeking to shift the discussion from the problems of disabled students to the ways in which institutions of higher education can design and implement policies and practices that ensure participation by students with disabilities, it focuses on ways of creating welcoming and encouraging campus environments for college students with disabilities. It discusses the paths that disabled students follow, the barriers that they face, and the actions that institutions can take to create barrier-free environments and help students achieve their goals. One of the most important goals of student services in postsecondary education is helping disabled people to achieve social and economic advancement through education, employment, and empowerment.

This volume is for practitioners—staff and managers who have responsibility for providing all students with services, including students with disabilities. It is for people who want to advance in the profession of disability and higher education, and, of course, it is for central administrators who have a legal and moral obligation to keep this topic on the agenda. The editors of this volume and the authors of its chapters are all involved in disability and higher education. They work in a variety of environments: large public research institutions, state universities, community colleges, public and private agencies. All have been guided in their efforts by a belief that the presence of disabled students can only enrich an academic institution and that an understanding of students with disabilities and their experiences on university and college campuses will significantly enhance the effort to diversify higher education.

In Chapter One, Jane Jarrow describes the history of disabled students in college. Students with disabilities have been part of our educational system for many years, but the awareness of their needs, the size and nature of the population, and the legal mandates for their inclusion have altered dramatically in the last twenty years. By tracing legal mandates and service programs and profiling disabled college students, Jarrow helps us to understand the philosophical issues and practical challenges that student service professionals have faced in their efforts to develop support services for disabled students in higher education.

In Chapter Two, Salome M. Heyward sketches a conceptual framework for the rights and responsibilities of students with disabilities in higher education. She reviews such issues as nondiscrimination, disclosure of disability, individualized assessment, qualified status, reasonable accommodation, documentation of disability, and confidentiality. To understand the legal mandates associated with disability and higher education, we must view these mandates as a series of competing rights and responsibilities. Heyward discusses students' rights and responsibilities in the context of a proper balancing of competing interests.

For students with disabilities, the movement from high school to adult life has been termed *transition* by parents, professionals, and recent legislation. In Chapter Three, Rhona C. Hartman presents a comprehensive picture of the transition to higher education by highlighting legislative mandates and model programs. She includes recommendations for student service professionals.

In Chapter Four, Kevin J. Nutter and Larry J. Ringgenberg review the literature on retention and "best" practices and apply it to disabled students. Traditionally, each new group that has entered higher education has been accompanied by a new group of student affairs practitioners charged with helping to meet its needs. The authors look at ecosystems theory, the literature on retention, and new roles for student affairs. Their discussion is focused on the roles that student affairs staff must play in the effort to integrate and involve students with disabilities in the university community.

The disability services offered on our college and university campuses vary widely in scope, sophistication, quality, and consistency. In Chapter Five, Judy Schuck and Sue Kroeger describe the components that a disability services office must have no matter what its size or configuration. After outlining critical program elements, the authors discuss the role of student services administrators. Throughout, they emphasize the need for coordination.

Students with learning disabilities form a growing population in higher education. Lydia S. Block focuses on these students in Chapter Six. She examines the most common definition of learning disability and reviews the common characteristics of learning-disabled (LD) students. Her discussion addresses several aspects of access for LD students, including identification, admissions, and academic accommodations. She examines the policy implications for student services personnel and makes recommendations for the future.

Students of color are significantly underrepresented in most college disability service programs. There are several reasons for this underrepresentation: cultural differences in the way in which disability is perceived, historical precedent, and language differences. Moreover, there is a double stigma in being identified both as "minority" and as "disabled." In Chapter Seven, Brenda Ball-Brown and Zelma Lloyd Frank discuss the barriers that disabled students of color face and the responses that they have developed. The authors outline some strategies for student services professionals.

In today's colleges and universities, instructional technology, computers, and education are joined in a powerful and complex relationship that is rapidly transforming our fundamental beliefs about the nature and process of instruction. In Chapter Eight, Carl Brown gives us an exciting glimpse of the roles that computers and technology are playing in efforts to eliminate disability-related barriers to education and employment. He shows how people with disabilities can become active partners in this evolving relationship.

Finally, in Chapter Nine, Sue Kroeger and Judy Schuck review the status of disabled students in college, identify salient issues, and recommend strategies that can help institutions of higher education to reach the goal of full participation.

The volume concludes in Chapter Ten with a comprehensive annotated review of resources for student services professionals, including the literature on disability and useful disability-related organizations.

The editors wish to express their appreciation to Anna Fellegy for her technical assistance and sense of humor; to Duyen Hong, Steve Chapman, and Richard Allegra for their input regarding disability services and students of color; and, of course, to their colleagues and families for their patience and support.

Sue Kroeger
Judy Schuck
Editors

SUE KROEGER is director of disability services at the University of Minnesota. Active in rehabilitation and higher education since 1975, she has published articles on disabled college students, taught college courses on disability studies, and delivered presentations at national and international conferences.

JUDY SCHUCK is associate dean of student services at Minneapolis Community College. In the last thirteen years, she has directed programs for students with disabilities in Minnesota and California, launched a statewide initiative on learning disabilities for the Minnesota Community College System, and served as a national trainer on learning disabilities for personnel in TRIO programs.

To understand the current state of disability and higher education,
we must first review the issues and challenges faced over the past
two decades.

Beyond Ramps: New Ways of Viewing Access

Jane Jarrow

Students with disabilities have been part of our educational system for many years, but the awareness of their needs, the size and nature of the population, and the legal mandates for their inclusion have changed dramatically in the last twenty years. To understand the nature of the services that are currently provided to students with disabilities, we must first understand the philosophical issues and practical challenges that the developers of disability support services as a component of student services in higher education have faced.

Historical Review

The history of students with disabilities in higher education is probably much longer than most people realize. The legislation that established federal funding for what is now Gallaudet University, the liberal arts institution for deaf students in Washington, D.C., was signed by Abraham Lincoln. More than 130 years ago, people in the United States recognized that an individual with a disability was not incapable of thinking, learning, or achieving. Nevertheless, for many of the hundred years that followed, students with disabilities were served at the whim of the institution that housed them, primarily as exceptions to the "typical" student population and largely as a result of unusual circumstances or through the efforts of unusual people.

Some institutions developed programs to address the unique needs of students with disabilities because someone with influence had reason to care. One of the larger institutions in New York City is rumored to have established a program for blind students many years ago because a faculty member had a son who was blind and wanted to attend college. This faculty member's colleagues knew the young man, knew that he had potential, and agreed that some arrangements could and should be made. Their response led to the establishment of an ongoing support program for blind students. Similarly, it is said that, even before Hawaii became a state, a Hawaiian legislator who became aware of the problems of blind students in college passed a bill allowing blind students to attend any institution of higher education in Hawaii tuition free; the money that the student saved could be used to pay readers.

In the late 1940s, Theodore Nugent, a faculty member in the rehabilitation counseling program at the University of Illinois, convinced the administration that the nation owed a debt to the many servicemen who returned from World War II in wheelchairs. Nugent set out to see that the opportunity to receive a college degree was available to these young men, and so was born one of the first deliberate efforts to create an architecturally barrier-free campus. The options for students in wheelchairs were for a long time quite limited. Most of the wheelchair users who graduated from college between the late 1940s and the mid 1960s attended one of the few institutions that made an issue of accessibility. These institutions included the University of Illinois, the University of Missouri, and Emporia State University. Those who attended other institutions tell stories of having been carried up stairs by fellow students throughout their college experience and of having been excluded from activities as often as they had been included.

In the 1960s, the notion that students with a variety of disabilities were ready and able to attend college acquired increasing viability. In the mid 1960s, Congress funded a number of exemplary programs across the country aimed at determining how best to fulfill the potential of disabled students. In 1968, the National Technical Institute for the Deaf was established in conjunction with the Rochester Institute of Technology in an effort to prepare for the influx of deaf students expected in postsecondary institutions as a result of the rubella epidemic of the early 1960s. This focus helped to set the stage for the large-scale disability rights issues that were about to be played out on the national stage.

The Rehabilitation Act of 1973 and Section 504

Congress passed the Rehabilitation Act in 1973. This legislation funded vocational rehabilitation agencies and activities throughout the United States. (It was reauthorized in 1992.) In 1973, Congress exceeded its previous mandates regarding services and support for people with disabilities by including in the act a subsection that is often viewed as the first national civil rights legislation for people with disabilities in the United States. (Several states had already instituted such legislation.) Section 504 of the Rehabilitation Act of 1973 stated that "no otherwise qualified individual with a disability in the United

States . . . shall, solely by reason of disability, be excluded from participation in, be denied the benefits of, or be subjected to discrimination under any program or activity receiving federal financial assistance" (29 U.S.C. 794).

This wording, which echoed that of preceding federal civil rights legislation regarding racial, ethnic, and gender discrimination (the Civil Rights Act of 1964 and the Title IX regulations that prohibited discrimination on the basis of gender), held out the promise of equal access under federal law to a population that hitherto had been served primarily at the convenience of others. The fight for civil rights for persons with disabilities differed from earlier battles in one important respect. Whereas the earlier struggles had culminated in formal recognition of the civil rights of the group concerned, the disability community found that passage of the act was only the beginning of its fight.

After passage of the Rehabilitation Act, many of the entities that were deemed to be covered by its provisions became concerned about the cost of the services that it mandated. In response to these concerns, the Nixon administration issued an executive order requiring a study of the consequences of Section 504 for federally funded activities. Implementation guidelines for Section 504 were not to be issued until this executive order had been fulfilled.

In fall 1976, the disability community was still waiting to see the protections promised by Section 504. Public hearings had been held, and tentative implementation guidelines had been drafted, but the Nixon and Ford administrations had done nothing to put the guidelines into effect. Disability rights advocates filed a class action lawsuit to force the federal government to release the guidelines. Late in November 1976, the federal courts ruled in favor of the plaintiffs, ordering the guidelines to be released. By that time, a new president had been elected, and a new administration was on its way to Washington. The Ford administration asked the court to postpone the issuance of guidelines until the new administration had taken office. The court agreed.

Carter administration officials, reviewing the regulations that their predecessors had developed, became concerned about the possible costs involved. The regulations were withheld for review. When it was announced that the regulations would not be released until the new administration had had an opportunity to study them, disability rights advocates organized a series of highly visible and vocal protests that culminated, late in March 1977, in a sit-in in the Region IX Office of the U.S. Department of Health, Education, and Welfare (DHEW) in San Francisco. Joseph Califano, secretary of DHEW, was visiting when more than a hundred individuals in wheelchairs invaded the office, chained themselves together, and insisted that they would not leave until they had seen the promise of Section 504 of the Rehabilitation Act fulfilled.

On March 28, Joseph Califano issued the Section 504 regulations from the San Francisco office. At the accompanying press conference, Califano was asked about the cost of implementation. His response has become the standard answer of disability advocates whenever the issue of cost is raised: "We have never before put a price tag on the cost of civil rights in this country. We do not intend to start now."

For the estimated forty-three million people with disabilities in the United States, Section 504 means more than access to opportunity. It holds out the promise of dignity in pursuit of the basic rights of safety and independence. Prior to Section 504, the provision of services and support for people with disabilities was largely the result of whim—pity, guilt, or obligation. Section 504 recognized that the functional limitations engendered by disability did not diminish the individual's status as a person whose right to life, liberty, and the pursuit of happiness is guaranteed by law.

Subpart E of Section 504 addresses the rights of people with disabilities in federally funded institutions of postsecondary education. These institutions include public and private institutions that receive federal grants or contracts and institutions with students who attend school with the help of guaranteed student loans or other forms of federal assistance. Since 1977, the number of students with disabilities who attend postsecondary institutions has risen dramatically. Service and support programs have been developed to enhance their experience, and the nature of the issues that influence inclusion has undergone several important changes.

Students with Disabilities in Higher Education

Section 504 defines *person with a disability* as anyone who has a substantial limitation in one or more of life's daily activities, including, but not limited to, walking, sleeping, eating, breathing, and learning. The fact that some disability populations are defined by law as part of the group of people with disabilities and thus entitled to nondiscrimination under the law does not necessarily mean that all individuals who have such limitations consider themselves to be disabled or choose to avail themselves of the support and services to which they are entitled by law. This right to choose is one of the most important tenets of Section 504: Students are not disabled unless they choose to consider themselves as such. Students have the right to accommodation, but they are also responsible for requesting such accommodation. The postsecondary institution is obligated to provide accommodation (that is, the appropriate support and services) only if the student requests them. Students with disabilities receive no special consideration or services until they ask for them.

That Section 504 emphasizes the similarities and not the differences between students with disabilities and their nondisabled peers reflects its civil rights nature, but it may have two unanticipated consequences. First, the philosophical framework for service and support is rooted in the views of equality and human rights held by the majority of Western culture. The services and support that result from this framework may not work as effectively for or be as open to participation by people from other cultural backgrounds. Second, by making students with disabilities part of the postsecondary student body, the legislation leaves no agency or entity charged with the task of determining the number of students with disabilities currently enrolled in higher education. Thus, our knowledge of the students with disabilities enrolled in higher education is based on limited, interpolated data.

The most complete data that we have both on the types of students with disabilities in higher education and on the growth in numbers of disabled students since Section 504 was implemented come from the annual survey conducted by the American Council on Education (HEATH Resource Center, 1992). This survey, which has included a question about disability status since 1978, is based on self-reports by full-time freshman students at the beginning of their college experience. The survey instrument does not define or explain the terms used to describe disability, and misinterpretation of the information sought may thus create some statistical artifacts. For example, a student who wears glasses that correct her vision to normal may still report a visual impairment, or a student for whom English is a second language may be moved by language differences to report a speech impairment.

Between 1978 and 1991, the percentage of entering freshmen reporting a disability rose from 2.6 percent to 8.8 percent, a figure that has been estimated to represent more than 140,000 freshmen across the United States. In 1985, the survey began to ask students to identify the type or types of disability that they had. The only dramatic increase in the type of disability reported has come in the area of learning disability: The percentage reporting such disability doubled in the six years between 1985 and 1991 from 1.1 to 2.2 percent. As noted later in this chapter, it is likely that the percentage increase would have been even larger if statistics had been available since Section 504 was first implemented.

Anecdotal evidence from service providers indicates some concerns about the type of disability reported. The discrepancies may be explained by the self-report nature of the information. First, the percentage of students with a degree of visual loss severe enough to be a substantial limitation and thus requiring some form of active accommodation at the postsecondary level is smaller than the figures indicate. According to service providers, only 5 to 10 percent of the students whom they serve have visual impairments. Second, the percentage of students with documented learning disabilities is higher than the 25 percent indicated by the survey. This discrepancy may result from the fact that students are not recognized to be learning-disabled (LD) until they have enrolled. Campuses that serve large numbers of students with disabilities other than learning disabilities indicate that their LD population still accounts for 35 to 50 percent of the students served. On campuses where the number of other-than-learning-disabled students is low, the percentage of LD students can range as high as 75 percent of the population served. Third, students served exclusively as a result of a speech impairment form the smallest category. While this number is very small—0.5 percent—it may be inflated by the number of students whose multiple disabilities include speech impairment or by students who equate language differences with disability.

The Mandate of Section 504

In order to carry out the mandate of Section 504, colleges and universities across the country have established offices to provide or coordinate reasonable accommodations for students with disabilities. The focus of these efforts has changed over time, but the basic philosophy under which they operate has not. From their inception, such offices have existed to ensure that students with disabilities have equal access to educational opportunities. Section 504 was never intended to be an extension of the special education statutes that govern service to students with disabilities in the K–12 system. It does not require institutions to establish separate educational programming or to provide any type or level of service that they do not already provide to nondisabled students on campus. It simply mandates that, if an opportunity is available to any student, it must be available to all students, regardless of disability. Section 504 is a program access statute. This means that it does not require all facilities used to be architecturally accessible. Instead, it requires all programs to be offered in architecturally accessible locations. Following this philosophy, it is relatively easy to determine the type of support that is covered under the law.

Section 504 mandates access to facilities and activities. If other students can participate simply by being present, students with disabilities must also be able to participate simply by being present. Classroom buildings, residence facilities, and student activity centers must be accessible whenever possible, and activities should be moved to accessible facilities if physical barriers in existing structures cannot be eliminated.

Section 504 mandates that admissions policies and practices may not discriminate on the basis of disability. An institution may not set arbitrary limits on the numbers of students with disabilities that it can accept. Moreover, an institution may not use a test that has been shown to discriminate against people with disabilities as the sole basis of determination. Thus, an institution may not use a cutoff score on a nationally standardized test, such as the SAT, the ACT, or the GRE, to screen out potential applicants with disabilities.

Section 504 mandates that testing procedures must accommodate students' disabilities. Classroom tests must be given in such a way that they test a disabled student's knowledge of course content, not the student's disability. Thus, Section 504 requires alterations in the presentation of test materials (by making them available in braille or large print or by having them read aloud or presented on tape), in the method of response (through use of word processing or a scribe), or in the length of time allowed for completing the examination. The examples just presented are all considered appropriate accommodations. Such accommodations are required under Section 504 on an as-needed basis.

Section 504 mandates the provision of such auxiliary aids and services as braille, large print, sign language interpreters, and adaptive equipment. The law does not require an institution to pay for such aids and services but only to make these accommodations available to students as needed at no cost. For example, if a student is eligible for services through the vocational rehabilitation system, an institution can require the student to seek payment for readers or interpreters from that system before assuming the responsibility itself.

Section 504 does not mandate the provision of personal care and other services. The institution does not help nondisabled students to dress, feed, or care for themselves, and it is not required to help students with disabilities in these areas, even if the student needs such services in order to participate fully in the programs that the institution makes available. Similarly, the institution is not required to provide equipment, such as a hearing aid or wheelchair, that the student uses in other situations as well as the educational setting, nor must it provide readers, scribes, or adaptive equipment used for personal study. (The institution must provide a reader if one is necessary so that the student can take a test. It is not required to provide the student with a reader to prepare for the examination.)

Section 504 may or may not mandate counseling and advising, priority scheduling, adaptive transportation and housing, and other such services. If an institution provides an activity or service for nondisabled students on campus, it must provide the activity or service for disabled students as well. For example, if the institution does not have a transportation system in place for students, it is under no obligation to establish such a system for disabled students. However, if the institution provides either fixed-route or special function transportation for students, it must assure that comparable transportation options are provided for people whose disabilities do not permit them to use the existing vehicles. If the institution issues parking permits to students and has designated areas for parking by students, then the institution must issue disability parking permits as needed and designate appropriate spaces for such use.

Section 504 may or may not mandate the provision of tutoring services. Usually it does not. If the institution makes tutoring services available to all students on campus free of charge, Section 504 requires it to make such services available to students with disabilities free of charge. If the institution limits the number of hours of tutoring per week that nondisabled students may receive, an appropriate accommodation may be to extend that limit and make additional hours of tutoring available to students with disabilities. However, if the institution does not make free tutoring available on demand to nondisabled students, it is not obligated to provide such a service to a student with disabilities, even if he or she needs it in order to compete successfully in the academic program.

Organization and Philosophy of Disability Support Service Programs

The role of service providers for students with disabilities in higher education has become a legitimate and viable specialty area within student services. The reader needs to remember that this new field grew not from the established discipline of rehabilitation, which focuses on changing the individual so that he or she is better able to cope with his or her environment, or from the field of special education, which emphasizes therapy and remediation, but from postsecondary student services, which finds its philosophical basis in empowerment and the maximization of potential and its legal mandates in equalization of opportunity.

The earliest attempts to provide for the needs of students with disabilities on campus came from centralized programs, in which all necessary support and service emanated from an office dedicated to those functions. The University of Illinois program had such an orientation; it provided or coordinated all the services necessary for students with disabilities. The Kokua Program at the University of Hawaii-Manoa (*kokua* means helper) has existed for more than twenty-five years. It, too, began at a time when the needs of students with disabilities were either met through the program or not at all. When Section 504 was implemented, institutions began to ask whether true equalization of opportunity could be fostered by decentralizing services for students with disabilities. If you needed a disability parking sticker, why not go to the campus police? That is what a nondisabled student who needed a parking sticker would do. If you needed advice on your academic schedule for the coming term, why not go to the same faculty advisers whom other students used? This approach seemed to work in some instances but not in others. Students with disabilities could be held responsible for disclosing their disability in order to obtain good advice in course selection or career direction. But whom would a disabled student approach if a class had to be moved to an accessible location or if a faculty member refused to allow a reasonable accommodation in class?

Focus on Programmatic Access

The field of disability services generally recognizes three types of barriers to the full inclusion of persons with disabilities: architectural barriers, attitudinal barriers, and programmatic barriers. While the removal of architectural barriers may have the highest price tag of the three, it is often the easiest to implement, because the need is generally obvious, and the solutions are fairly clear. If a student in a wheelchair needs access to the second floor of a building, you know you must find a way of getting the student there. Attitudinal barriers are much more difficult to deal with. While the eradication of such barriers has a low or no price tag, it is often the most difficult to achieve, because attitudinal barriers are hard to isolate clearly. Too often attitudinal barriers are the result of an individual's honest (although mistaken) concern for protecting the person with a disability from harm or disappointment or from the belief that people with disabilities will be happier with "their own kind." Programmatic barriers to access fall somewhere in between. They may or may not be obvious in nature, cost money to eliminate, and be easy to eradicate.

Section 504 has always mandated programmatic rather than architectural access. However, compliance in the first years after implementation seemed to focus on the removal of physical barriers to participation. Proponents of such efforts reasonably argued that, if a campus lacked a basic level of architectural access, then the kinds of efforts that were needed to produce equal access programmatically were also unlikely. Moreover, it was felt that the individuals who were most likely to seek higher education once they had the opportunity to do so would be those who were blind, deaf, or in a wheelchair. While all individuals with disabilities as defined by the law were entitled to free access, the people who had campaigned for the opportunity were primarily those with visible disabilities or those whose disability had visible concomitants. What they needed, for the most part, was architectural access.

A review of the early literature on postsecondary disability support services underlines this emphasis on physical access. Articles on adaptive housing and transportation systems were prevalent. Checklists for architectural compliance and options for creating physical access were offered. While very little of the literature dealt with programmatic access, it did seem to recognize that attitudes needed to change if students were to be successful, and a great deal of the literature centered on sensitivity and awareness training for faculty and staff regarding the needs and potential of people with disabilities. As long as most accommodations did not involve direct intervention in the way in which classes were conducted (as by changing a room assignment to ensure wheelchair access, or arranging for an interpreter, or providing course materials in braille or on tape), faculty involvement was felt to consist in attitudinal support for the efforts of students with disabilities to achieve at the level of nondisabled peers. This is not to say that there were not early struggles to establish the right of a student to bring a guide dog into class or to tape-record a lecture as an alternative to taking notes. However, if the faculty member could be convinced that the legislation was basically civil rights in nature and if the faculty member believed in maximizing student potential, most arguments came down to education about the appropriateness of the accommodation, not about the need for accommodation.

In the early 1980s, increasing numbers of students with learning disabilities found their way onto college campuses across the country. Few disability service providers were prepared for this influx. The general belief seems to have been that learning disabilities existed in children and that they affected formal K–12 educational processes; if the special education system worked properly, such students would have learned so well to cope with their disabilities by the time they reached college that no accommodations would have to be made. In retrospect, we can see that this belief was foolish. Because they are neurological in origin, learning disabilities are permanent in nature. We should have realized that children with learning disabilities grow up to be adults with learning disabilities. Moreover, since we know that learning disabilities have no effect on an individual's intellectual potential, we should have expected a large number of otherwise qualified students with learning disabilities to want to pursue higher education. Nevertheless, the steadily increasing number of students with learning disabilities in higher education has challenged service providers to define appropriate accommodations and given postsecondary educators new concerns in determining how best to provide programmatic access to educational opportunities.

Case Law and Legislative Mandates

In contrast, the determination of accommodations that were appropriate for individuals with physical or sensory disabilities was much easier. The nature of such disabilities is better understood. The first Supreme Court challenge to Section 504 (*Southeastern Community College* v. *Davis*, 1979) involved a potential nursing student with a severe hearing impairment who had been denied enrollment in a training program involving clinical placements in intensive care settings and operating rooms in which the potential student could not participate effectively or safely. She sued for the right to have the portions of the program that were impossible for her to complete eliminated or de-emphasized. The court found that the college was not responsible for making substantial changes in an essential element of the curriculum; the student could be denied access in this case. It is much easier to determine that a request for programmatic access can be denied when the disability directly affects the skill or task that is being evaluated (as it does when the student must lip-read through a surgical mask).

The influx of students with learning disabilities caused great confusion among postsecondary educators about appropriate accommodation and programmatic access. When a student knows the correct answers to all the questions on a history test but cannot read the questions independently as the result of a learning disability, how does the institution best provide programmatic access to the history class? If the student is a wonderful counselor in one-to-one circumstances and has the potential to be an outstanding social worker but is prevented by a math disability from passing the core requirement college algebra class, how does the institution provide the student with programmatic access to a degree in social work?

While postsecondary institutions still struggle with the answers and occasionally argue for restrictions, the courts have in recent years been consistent in their consideration of such matters. Students are to be considered otherwise qualified if they meet the essential requirements of the program with or without appropriate accommodation. The definition and limits of appropriate accommodation have been and continue to be tested in the courts and under rulings from the federal Office of Civil Rights. Section 504 is not very specific on this topic. Some view that as its greatest weakness; others, as its greatest strength. It is not always possible to refer to a legally enforceable document that unambiguously states what must be done. However, by leaving the determination of *appropriate* jointly to service providers, educators, and consumers, Congress has limited the possibilities for accommodation only to the limits of our ingenuity. It is impossible to meet the letter of this law without also meeting its spirit.

As service providers have become increasingly involved in negotiating and arranging accommodations that affect classroom activities directly—accommodations ranging from the provision of notetakers to alternate media, extended time on tests, and distraction-free settings—it has become increasingly clear that institutions need someone outside the teaching faculty to maintain primary responsibility for such arrangements. Most disability support service programs today follow a kind of modified centralized model. Any services that can be provided outside the office—services ranging from parking stickers to career counseling by trained individuals—are provided outside the office. The central office focuses on documenting the need for students seeking accommodation, determining reasonable accommodations, and providing the support services, liaison activities, and advocacy that students cannot accomplish individually.

Of the many cases that have had a significant impact on the way in which the needs and rights of students with disabilities are viewed on college campuses, it is appropriate to mention *Brown v. Washington University* (1990). The student who brought the suit used a wheelchair, and the primary complaints involved the lack of physical access on campus. In finding for the plaintiff in this case, the court stated that the institution had a responsibility to be proactive in meeting the needs of qualified students with disabilities on its campus and that the student should never have had to bring the suit; someone within the system should have had the responsibility for advocating on behalf of disabled students. As part of the settlement, the university was required to establish an office of disabled student services.

Americans with Disabilities Act

On July 25, 1990, President Bush signed into law the Americans with Disabilities Act (ADA). This law extends the mandate for nondiscrimination on the basis of disability to the private sector and the nonfederal public sector, that is, to state and local government. Covering employment and public accommodations as well as higher education, the ADA is generally considered to be the most sweeping piece of civil rights legislation passed in more than twenty-five years. Title II of the ADA covers community colleges and state institutions; Title III covers private institutions. Chapter Two of this volume discusses the ADA in some detail. The reader needs to remember that Section 504 of the Rehabilitation Act of 1973 is still in effect for entities that receive federal funds. Thus, most colleges and universities in the United States are subject both to Section 504 and to the ADA. Thus, the ADA is likely to have its greatest impact on higher education by increasing awareness of the existence and needs of the people in our society with disabilities.

On signing the ADA, President George Bush stated that we must eliminate the architectural and attitudinal barriers that we have created and allowed.

The renewed focus on civil rights and equal opportunities for people with disabilities reminds us that people with disabilities are more like other people than they are different. In this way, they are like the kiwi bird, which has wings but cannot fly. What "bird things" does the kiwi bird do if it cannot fly? All the other things, of course.

References

Brown v. *Washington University* (CA No. 88–1907–C–5, 1990).

HEATH Resource Center. *American Freshman: National Norms*. Washington, D.C.: American Council on Education, 1992.

Southeastern Community College v. *Davis*, 1979.

JANE JARROW, *executive director of the Association on Higher Education and Disability (AHEAD), is known nationally for her publications and presentations on college students with disabilities.*

The key to compliance with disability discrimination laws is balancing the rights of disabled individuals with the institution's desire to preserve the integrity of its programs.

Students' Rights and Responsibilities

Salome M. Heyward

The Americans with Disabilities Act (ADA) and Section 504 of the Rehabilitation Act of 1973 impose a responsibility on postsecondary institutions not to discriminate on the basis of disability and to provide disabled individuals with meaningful access. The ADA mirrors the general compliance mandates of Section 504, but Section 504 contains specific regulatory provisions regarding the delivery of services to students. While most of us have little difficulty understanding the legal mandates on a theoretical level, we often lose our way when we attempt to make them work in the real world, and what-ifs and legalese can raise some troubling questions. For example, does an institution's responsibility to provide access require it to waive or substitute a course or program requirement? Can a disabled student limit an institution's ability to use the information that he or she provides in support of a request for academic adjustments? What is the difference between reasonable accommodation and a fundamental alteration to the educational program? To what extent can students be held accountable for ensuring access? Is it possible for an institution to comply with the legal mandate to provide meaningful access and still maintain its academic integrity?

Questions like these are threatening to turn interactions between disabled students and postsecondary institutions into something like open warfare. Students charge that institutions are unresponsive to their needs and seek actively to avoid their responsibilities under the law, while institutions counter that students' requests go well beyond the requirements of the regulations and refuse to accept the responsibilities that the regulations impose on them. Who is right? The truth is that both sides are a little bit right and a little bit wrong. Parties are arguing that there are absolute rights and responsibilities where there are no absolutes. The Supreme Court held in 1985 that the key to compliance with disability discrimination laws lies in the obligation to balance the right of disabled individuals to be "integrated into the society [with] the legitimate interest of the federal grantees in preserving the integrity of their programs" (*Alexander* v. *Choate*, 1985, at 300–301). Thus, to understand the proper relationship of the parties with respect to the legal mandates, we must begin by viewing these mandates as a series of competing rights and responsibilities. There is always a continuum. The analysis in this chapter focuses on the factors that tip the balance in favor of one party or the other. This chapter discusses students' rights and responsibilities in terms of the proper balance between competing interests:

Rights	Responsibilities
Nondiscrimination, meaningful access	Request "reasonable" modification
Individualized assessments	Meet eligibility standards for qualified status
Effective academic adjustments, aids	Provide documentation
Confidentiality	Provide necessary information

Meaningful Access, Reasonable Modifications

Institutions have two primary responsibilities: They must not discriminate against qualified disabled individuals, and they must give these individuals meaningful access to the services, benefits, and programs that they offer. The regulatory mandates require institutions both to treat disabled individuals as they do similarly situated nondisabled individuals and to address the unique differences of disabled individuals. The prohibition against discrimination requires that qualified disabled individuals be given the same opportunities as all other students to participate in and benefit from the programs offered. Thus, it would be unlawful discrimination not to allow a student who has excellent credentials and who meets established admissions requirements to enroll in a program solely because he has multiple sclerosis (*Pushkin* v. *Regents of the University of Colorado*, 1981). However, disabled students often cannot be given such opportunities unless the institution modifies its programs, policies, practices, or procedures (*Lau* v. *Nichol*, 1974). The Supreme Court describes the responsibility to provide access in these terms: "It is possible to envision situations where an insistence on continuing past requirements and practices might arbitrarily deprive genuinely qualified handicapped persons of the opportunity to participate in a covered program. . . . Thus, situations may arise where a refusal to modify an existing program might become unreasonable and discriminatory" (*Southeastern Community College* v. *Davis*, 1979, at 411–413). To assure meaningful access, reasonable accommodations may have to be made in the grantee program or benefit (*Alexander* v. *Choate*, 1985).

As the court noted in *Wynne* v. *Tufts University School of Medicine* (1991, at 19), "there is a real obligation on the academic institution to seek suitable means of reasonably accommodating a handicapped person." Thus, a university cannot simply refuse to provide deaf students with interpreter services, deny auxiliary aids to students in nondegree programs, fail to accommodate mobility-impaired students in its business education laboratory, refuse to make a new swimming pool accessible to mobility-impaired students, or fail to give disabled individuals transportation services that are equal to or as effective as those offered to nondisabled individuals (*United States of America* v. *Board of Trustees for the University of Alabama*, 1990). In the case just cited, the court upheld the validity of the enforcement agency's mandate that educational institutions are responsible for providing disabled students with auxiliary aids and equivalent services. The court specifically noted that in "some instances the lack of an auxiliary aid effectively denies a handicapped student equal access to his or her opportunity to learn" (*United States of America* v. *Board of Trustees for the University of Alabama*, 1990, at 748).

The student's right to meaningful access is clear and unquestionable, but just how sweeping is this right, and how heavy is the institution's burden of responsibility? In *Southeastern Community College* v. *Davis* (1979) and in *Alexander* v. *Choate* (1985), the Supreme Court established the test for determining whether the proposed modifications can be classified as reasonable accommodations and therefore as necessary for the provision of meaningful access. Simply put, institutions are required to take actions that can be characterized as reasonable accommodations; they are not required to take actions that can be classified as affirmative action in scope. The court held that

> Section 504 by its terms does not compel educational institutions to disregard the disabilities of handicapped individuals or to make substantial modifications to their programs. (*Southeastern Community College* v. *Davis*, 1979, at 405)

> [N]either the language, purpose, nor history of 504 reveals an intent to impose an affirmative-action obligation. (*Southeastern Community College* v. *Davis*, 1979, at 411)

> [A]ffirmative action referred to those "changes," "adjustments," or "modifications" to existing programs that would be "substantial" . . . or that would constitute "fundamental alteration[s]" in the nature of the program . . . rather than to those changes that would be reasonable accommodations. (*Alexander* v. *Choate*, 1985, at 300–301)

> [W]hile a grantee need not be required to make "fundamental or substan-
> tial" modifications . . . , it may be required to make "reasonable" ones. . . .
> (*Alexander* v. *Choate,* 1985, at 300–301)

The court also noted that institutions are not required to take actions that impose undue administrative or financial burdens. The task of determining whether a requested modification should be classified as affirmative action or as reasonable accommodation is often not easy to make. Even the Supreme Court acknowledged that distinguishing between the two can be difficult: "We do not suggest that the line between a lawful refusal to extend affirmative action and illegal discrimination against handicapped persons always will be clear" (*Southeastern Community College* v. *Davis,* 1979, at 412).

A number of proposed modifications have been held to be affirmative action in nature and thus beyond an institution's obligation to provide meaningful access: altering the clinical portion of a nursing program to eliminate the requirement that the student perform independently without supervision (*Southeastern Community College* v. *Davis,* 1979); eliminating technical proficiency skills that had been adopted as part of the professional standards for optometry (*Doherty* v. *Southern School of Optometry,* 1988); readmitting a law student with a drinking problem who had been readmitted on three other occasions and who failed to meet the school's standards for acceptable performance (*Anderson* v. *University of Wisconsin,* 1988); readmitting to medical school a student with chronic psychiatric and mental disorders who had a history of suicide attempts and physical attacks on nurses and doctors (*Doe* v. *New York University,* 1981); admitting a student who was HIV-positive to dental school (*Doe* v. *Washington University,* 1991); altering a test format in a situation where the institution could establish on the one hand that it had already provided the student with numerous other accommodations (for example, tutoring, allowing the student to retake the first-year curriculum, conducting makeup exams in untimed settings) and on the other hand that multiple-choice examinations offered a "superior means to evaluate student performance," while oral examinations were "not feasible and too subjective" (*Wynne* v. *Tufts University School of Medicine,* 1992).

In each of the cases just cited, the courts decided that the proposed modifications were either substantial, fundamental alterations or that they posed undue financial and administrative burdens. Only refusals to implement modifications that do not rise to these levels will be considered unreasonable and discriminatory denials of access. Students often fail either to comprehend or to acknowledge that the responsibility to provide access is not limitless. There is a line, and under the law it is substantial. That line is a "continuum in which some modest modifications may be necessary to avoid discrimination but other more substantial modifications are not required" (*Americans Disabled for Accessible Public Transportation* v. *Skinner,* 1989, at 1192).

Individualized Assessment, Qualified Status

Only disabled individuals who are qualified are entitled to protection under Section 504 and the ADA. On the continuum, this means that institutions have a responsibility to provide meaningful access to qualified disabled individuals, that disabled individuals must meet legitimate eligibility standards and criteria, and that disabled individuals have a right to an individualized assessment of their skills and abilities regarding the determination of their qualified status.

How does one identify these qualified individuals? Most institutions have difficulty with this question, and the regulations have not answered it clearly. "There is no bright line separating those who are 'qualified' and those who are not" (*Rhone v. United States Department of Army*, 1987, at 745 n.19). As the preceding discussion suggests, this question can be answered appropriately only by addressing the issue on two distinct levels: the limitations, if any, imposed by the disability and the legitimacy of the eligibility criteria standards.

The primary problem lies in determining the considerations that are legitimate when viewing the limitations imposed by a disability. The Supreme Court has made a number of important pronouncements in this regard. First, a qualified individual is "one who can meet all of the program requirements in spite of his handicap" (*Southeastern Community College v. Davis*, 1979, at 406). Second, physical qualification may be considered necessary for meeting the eligibility requirements of a program or essential to performance (*Southeastern Community College v. Davis*, 1979). Third, the question of whether a person is qualified requires "an individualized inquiry" (*Arline v. School Board of Nassau County*, 1987, at 287). Fourth, "the question of who is 'otherwise qualified' and what actions constitute 'discrimination'. . . would seem to be two sides of a single coin; the ultimate question is the extent to which a grantee is required to make reasonable modifications" (*Alexander v. Choate*, 1985, at 299).

"Section 504 does not compel educational institutions to disregard the disabilities of handicapped individuals" (*Southwestern Community College v. Davis*, 1979, at 405, 410–412). Thus, the court concluded in the case just cited the ability to hear was essential to successful performance in the nursing clinical program under consideration. However, disabilities must be considered on an individualized basis. The institution must consider the individual skills and abilities of the disabled person. An institution may not exclude disabled individuals on the basis of general perceptions of the limitations imposed by a particular impairment. "Mere possession of a handicap is not a permissible ground for assuming an inability to function in a particular context" (*Doe v. Region 13 Mental Retardation Commission*, 1983, at 1402). The mandate for individualized inquiry is indeed powerful. In one recent case, the state of Alabama was found to be in violation of the Rehabilitation Act because it had enforced a blanket policy of isolation and segregation for prison inmates who had AIDS or who were HIV positive. Such inmates were denied the right to interact with the general prison population in all programs and activities. The state was ordered to conduct individualized inquiries to determine the risk of transmission not merely with respect to the general population but also for each program and activity (*Harris v. Thigpen,* 1991). In *Arline v. School Board of Nassau County* (1987), the Supreme Court stated that the primary purpose of statutes and regulations prohibiting discrimination on the basis of disability is to eliminate the exclusion of entire groups of disabled individuals on the basis of general perceptions of the limitations imposed by particular impairments, unfounded fears, or remote possibilities.

Does the fact that one disability prevents an individual from meeting all program requirements from the very outset end the inquiry? In *Brennan v. Stewart* (1988), a blind individual had been denied a temporary hearing aid training permit because licensure regulations required applicants to perform otoscopic examinations and ear impression. It had been presumed that blindness would preclude the individual from meeting that standard. The court ruled that, while the requirement was reasonable, the individual could not be denied the opportunity to demonstrate that reasonable accommodations could be made to permit him to meet the standard. Thus, a qualified disabled individual is an individual who with reasonable accommodation can meet the essential qualifications or criteria for participation in the services, program, or activities in question.

Institutions often view the mandate to provide reasonable accommodations as an infringement on their academic integrity. That is, it either prohibits them from using eligibility standards and criteria, or it requires them to lower the standards applied to disabled individuals. Such views are the product of the belief or feeling that the mere presence of a disability prevents an individual from performing at the level of nondisabled individuals. The regulations do not preclude or interfere with the right of institutions to impose and enforce acceptable criteria and standards. The courts and the federal enforcement agencies neither desire nor are qualified to step into the shoes of educators and those who administer postsecondary educational programs. Educators set such standards. "The four essential freedoms of a university are to determine for itself on academic grounds: a) who may teach, b) what may be taught, c) how it shall be taught, d) and who may be admitted to study" (*Sweezy v. New Hampshire,* 1957, at 263). If the criteria, standards, and requirements that screen out disabled individuals are legitimate, reasonable, essential, and related in rational ways to the program's goals and purposes, they will be upheld.

Are institutions required to waive criteria and standards that disabled individuals cannot meet even with accommodations? What is a university's responsibility to a student with a learning disability who has been provided accommodations, such as tutoring and extended time on tests, and who cannot meet the foreign language requirement necessary for graduation? Neither the courts nor the federal enforcement agencies have responded favorably to requests that eligibility criteria and standards be waived for disabled individuals. For example, in *Pandayides v. Virginia Board of Education* (1990), a teacher with a learning disability who was unable to pass the communications skills portion of the National Teacher Examination charged that the state's refusal to grant her a teaching certificate because she could not pass the examination was discriminatory and violated Section 504. She suffered from an attention deficit disorder and had difficulty processing auditory information. To accommodate her disability, the institution allowed her additional time on the test, but she asked for unlimited time or that the requirement be waived. The court concluded that, since it was legitimate for Virginia to require that teachers licensed to teach in the state demonstrate an ability to "understand and use the elements of written or spoken language," it could require the plaintiff to pass the examination as a condition for receiving a teacher's certificate (*Pandayides* v. *Virginia Board of Education*, 752 F. Supp. 696 (E.D. Va. 1990)). The court further noted that requiring the state either to waive the requirement or to provide unlimited time represented the type of substantial modification and fundamental alteration that is not required under Section 504. Both strategies went beyond nondiscrimination onto the territory of affirmative action.

Requiring disabled individuals to meet legitimate standards and criteria that are rationally related to the stated goals or purposes of a program does not violate the regulations. If the criteria and standards are legitimate and essential, there can be no justification for requiring nondisabled individuals to meet them while relieving similarly situated disabled individuals of the responsibility to do so.

It is often difficult for selective admissions programs and for programs that require participants to demonstrate the acquisition of particular skills or technical abilities to determine how best to assess the qualified status of applicants and participants. The best approach is to begin by reviewing program requirements and isolating the essential skills, abilities, and qualifications that all students must either possess or acquire. These standards should remain the same for everyone, and they should not be altered simply because there are disabled individuals who wish to participate in the program. Disabled individuals should not be required to meet higher standards or assume greater costs than nondisabled persons must bear in order to gain access to the services, benefits, or programs offered. Institutions also may not require disabled individuals to accept lesser services or benefits as a condition for participation. Six pertinent questions have to be answered regarding the assessment of qualified status. First, are the criteria or standards that are being used rationally related to the purposes of the program? Irrelevant factors, such as the student's ultimate employability, should not be used solely to disqualify disabled individuals. The issue is whether the individual is qualified to participate in the educational program. Second, are there other criteria or standards that would be equally effective and that would have a less adverse impact on disabled individuals? Third, is it legitimate to consider the individual's disability; that is, will the disability have an impact on the individual's performance or acquisition of the necessary skills and abilities? Fourth, can academic adjustments or reasonable accommodations be made that would permit the individual to participate? Fifth, have all relevant factors been considered in reaching the determination that the individual is not qualified? The right of the disabled individual to be included must be balanced against the right of the institution to protect the integrity of its program. Sixth, does the institution's decision-making process reflect that pertinent factors were considered in a more than cursory way and that legitimate reasons support the determinations? The refusal to accommodate cannot be arbitrary and capricious (*Southeastern Community College v. Davis*, 1979, at 411–413).

Effective Accommodation, Documentation

Institutions must do more than simply open their doors and tell qualified disabled individuals that they may enter. The obligation to provide meaningful access is not limited simply to "making the building and physical facilities accessible" (*Nathanson v. Medical College of Pennsylvania*, 1991, at 1368). Institutions must "seek suitable means of reasonably accommodating handicapped persons" to ensure that they have access to an opportunity to learn (*Wynne v. Tufts University School of Medicine*, 1992, at 16; *United States of America v. Board of Trustees for the University of Alabama*, 1990, at 746). As the court noted in *United States of America v. Board of Trustees for the University of Alabama* (1990), a deaf student with no interpreter is effectively denied meaningful access to a class, and all access to the benefits of some courses is eliminated.

Some hypothetical cases illustrate the challenges that determining whether to provide accommodation presents to institutions. Jane was classified as a learning-disabled student throughout her high school career. She requests auxiliary aids, but she provides no documentation for the existence of her disability. Bill provides documentation that is six years old. The evaluator states that Bill appears to have a learning disability and recommends that he be tutored in math. Bill requests extended test time and tutoring for all his classes. Sally presents the results of a complete battery of tests, which she took three months before she enrolled. The director of the handicapped student services (HSS) office admits that the evaluation data are complete and supports Sally's request for extended test time and a course substitution for the university's basic math requirement. However, because HSS has had difficulty convincing the math department to accommodate disabled students, the director asks Sally to agree to additional evaluation aimed at determining whether a program could be developed that would help her to pass the basic math requirement. Frank has a minor hearing impairment. Generally, the use of hearing aids corrects his hearing deficiency adequately, but he has difficulty with certain sounds and voice patterns. The evaluator recommends that Frank be provided with notetakers and states that he should also be provided with tutoring for his lecture courses. Jeff does not advise the institution that he needs academic adjustments until the day of the midterm examination. At that time, he demands extended test time.

The preceding hypothetical cases exemplify some of the most difficult questions that institutions face when they must determine whether they have a duty to make academic adjustments and provide auxiliary aids. What are the student's responsibilities? What additional information, if any, may the institution require the student to provide? When does the institution's responsibility to provide academic adjustments arise? What limits are there on the institution's obligation to provide academic adjustments?

Academic adjustments are the area in which disabled students have the greatest responsibilities. In contrast to students in elementary and secondary institutions, the students in postsecondary institutions share responsibility for the provision of appropriate academic adjustments with their institution. While the institution must give them information about its duty to provide academic adjustments and auxiliary aids and identify the persons who need to be contacted for these services, it is not required to provide accommodation until the student notifies the institution of his or her disability and needs, makes a request for accommodation, and provides documentation supporting the request. An institution has no obligation to accommodate needs that have not been brought to its attention or to provide accommodations that have not been requested (*Salvador v. Bell*, 1986). More important, institutions do not have a unilateral right to assess a student's needs or address them in the absence of some action or request from the student. But what form must this action or request take?

Nathanson v. Medical College of Pennsylvania (1991) shows how complicated the question of the institution's responsibility to act can become. In *Nathanson*, a woman with a back and neck impairment was granted admission to the Medical College of Pennsylvania (MCP). Although she denied in her preadmissions interview that she needed accommodation, she experienced serious back and neck pain once she started classes. She attributed the pain in large part to classroom seating arrangements. Citing the pain that she had experienced while trying to take notes for six to seven hours a day, she requested a leave of absence, which was granted. She did not ask for accommodation at that time but rather stated that she felt her physical condition would improve during the year. She would also investigate possible modifications that could be made to reduce the physical strain during classes. The evidence establishes that the student discussed her physical problems with school officials during the following year and advised them that she needed special seating arrangements. However, she also advised them that she was taking responsibility for obtaining a special chair. She further stated that her physical problems would prevent her from attending the school unless she could be accommodated. School officials contended that the student never directly requested specific accommodations. The Court of Appeals held that, in order to be liable under the Rehabilitation Act, the MCP must know or reasonably be expected to know of the student's handicap. Neither the Rehabilitation Act nor the regulations specify what kind of notification is necessary to inform an institution adequately of a person's handicap, nor do they define what constitutes awareness of a handicap.

Further, the court rejected the district court's finding that the student never made a "sufficiently direct and specific request for special accommodation" by noting that this fact would be relevant only if the school "neither knew nor had reason to know that Nathanson was handicapped" (*Nathanson* v. *Medical College of Pennsylvania*, 1991, at 1381). The key question is whether it would be reasonable under the circumstances to hold the institution accountable for failure to provide academic adjustments. Thus, a student who, like Jeff, failed to request academic adjustments until the date on which a test was scheduled is not entitled to immediate accommodation.

It is not sufficient for a student merely to request or demand academic adjustments. The student is responsible for providing documentation that supports the request. The documentation should establish clearly that the student has a disability as defined by the regulations, and it should provide sufficient information regarding manifestations of the disability to permit the institution to determine whether the accommodations requested are appropriate. If the documentation does not provide the necessary information, then the institution can legitimately ask the student to submit additional information, and it must have sufficient time and opportunity to investigate and clarify (*Nathanson* v. *Medical College of Pennsylvania*, 1991).

In the hypothetical cases sketched earlier, neither Jane nor Bill provided enough information that the university could make an informed decision regarding their right to receive accommodations or the form that such accommodation should take. However, Sally provided all the necessary information. Therefore, if the institution wants to take issue with the test results or if it wants further clarification, it must take full responsibility for paying for the additional evaluations and providing the accommodations in a timely fashion.

Students must accept their responsibility to provide adequate documentation, and institutions must provide adjustments in a timely fashion once such documentation has been provided. Institutions embroiled in controversy about the appropriateness or nature of accommodations often lose sight of their responsibility to take timely action. Unreasonable delays in the provision of accommodations as well as express denials will be closely scrutinized. If an institution makes it so difficult to obtain services that disabled individuals give up out of sheer frustration or must invest an inordinate amount of time and energy to obtain them, the institution may be charged with unlawful discrimination. For example, in *James* v. *Frank* (1991), the court concluded that a seven-month delay in providing a chair for an employee who was an amputee was not reasonable.

Both the federal enforcement agency and the courts have ruled that institutions are ultimately financially responsible for the provision of academic adjustments and auxiliary aids. Most recently, in *United States of America* v. *Board of the Trustees of the University of Alabama* (1990), the court ruled that the university's policy of applying a financial means test when auxiliary aids were requested violated Section 504. The present interpretation of the regulations precludes any policy that requires students to assume direct financial responsibility for necessary accommodations absent a showing of undue administrative or financial burden. Thus, institutions may not require students to use funds obtained from student loan programs to pay for accommodations.

Must a college or university honor a student's request to hire an interpreter of his or her own choice although that interpreter costs significantly more than the interpreters whom the institution has on staff? An institution's primary responsibility is to provide effective accommodations. Disabled individuals often believe mistakenly that the institution must supply the exact accommodation that they have requested or that their evaluation recommends. While an institution should not ignore students' suggestions and while it should involve them in discussions regarding potential accommodations and in assessments of their effectiveness, the institution ultimately has the right to choose the manner in which it provides meaningful access (*Carter* v. *Bennett*, 1988). As long as the accommodations chosen are effective and qualified disabled individuals are not excluded from the educational program, questions about compliance with the regulations will be resolved in the institution's favor.

Students also have the responsibility to provide for their own personal needs (for example, guide dogs, personal attendants, and wheelchairs) and to use the accommodations that the institution provides in an appropriate manner. They cannot behave irresponsibly with respect to the accommodations offered without facing the consequences. For example, a student who is verbally abusive to interpreters may be denied interpreter services if he or she refuses to behave in an appropriate manner. An institution may cease to provide a particular accommodation to a student under such circumstances.

Confidentiality, Necessary Information

There is a great deal of confusion about the individuals within an institution who should be privy to information that disabled students have provided about their identity and the nature of their disabilities. To understand this issue, we must keep the intent of the regulations in mind: Qualified disabled individuals should not be subjected to intrusive inquiries regarding their disabilities. Questions about the existence and impact of a disability should be asked only when the individual is seeking accommodation or the individual's qualified status is at issue. Further, Section 104.42 of the regulations limits the ways in which institutions can obtain and use such information. For example, it states that such information may be gathered only for purposes of providing accommodation, to remediate past discrimination, or to address past practices that limited the participation of a disabled individual. More important, such inquiries must be made on a confidential basis, and the information that is gathered must be kept confidential. The process has two key characteristics: its voluntary nature and its overall confidentiality. The disabled individual has the right to decide whether to make the information available to the institution, and the fact that he or she does so for purposes of accommodation does not entitle the institution to use the information for any other purposes thereafter. In other words, disclosure for the purposes of accommodation does not equal blanket permission. Thus, the disabled student services office may not give the admissions office a list of the names of disabled students unless it has the students' permission to do so. In the absence of such permission, it may only provide information about the number of students served, the types of disabilities, and the range of academic adjustments provided. Everything that would have allowed the students to be identified must have been removed.

Situations in which there is disagreement about the academic adjustments that should be provided present a slightly different problem. To whom may the disabled student services office disclose the information, and how much information should it disclose? In cases bearing directly on qualified status and accommodation, it is clear that the person or persons who have been appointed as arbiters of such disputes must have access to the information. As noted earlier, a student who asks for accommodation must provide documentation to support the request. With the request comes permission to consider the documentation received for that specific purpose.

However, the institution still has an important responsibility regarding confidentiality. Access to the information must be limited to those involved in the deliberation process, and the data to which they have access must be limited to the specific questions at issue. For example, if Bill, who has a visual impairment and a history of stress-related disorders, is seeking accommodation only for his visual impairment, the arbiters have no need for the information regarding the stress-related disorders.

Similarly, if the only question is which in a series of academic adjustments is the most appropriate and if the existence of the disability is not at issue, only information that relates to the academic adjustments issue needs to be provided. Information relating to the existence of the disability may properly be withheld. However, as noted earlier, institutions are not required to ignore evidence of the existence of disabilities that raise questions about an individual's qualified status. If a student shows signs of disability, behaves inappropriately, or has difficulty performing, it may be appropriate for the institution to initiate discussions with the student concerning his or her ability to function in the program.

Conclusion

Issues regarding the delivery of services to students on the postsecondary level are becoming increasingly complicated. The center of controversy has moved from the relatively simple questions of whether academic adjustments should be provided to more complicated and troubling questions of what, how, and in what form they should be provided. There are no easy answers to these questions, and the parties often make resolution more difficult by viewing each controversy as a win-or-lose situation. They must remember that, for every right that a student or an institution has, there is a corresponding responsibility. Major issues or controversies are better resolved through negotiation and compromise than through confrontation. Successful resolutions are the product of a participatory process in which all parties accept responsibility for developing solutions that provide opportunities for individuals with disabilities while maintaining the integrity of the programs and services offered.

The participants in such a process would do well to remember the following important principles: First, there are few absolutes. Balancing is the key. Second, institutions must provide meaningful access. Meaningful access does not mean fundamental alterations to programs or services or modifications that impose undue financial or administrative burdens. Third, disabled individuals must meet legitimate program requirements, standards, and criteria. Fourth, an individualized assessment must be conducted to establish qualified status. Fifth, a qualified disabled individual is one who can meet essential qualifications and criteria with or without reasonable accommodations. Sixth, an institution has a duty to take action when officials know or should have known of the individual's disability and potential need. Seventh, a disabled individual has a duty to support a request for accommodation with adequate documentation and to use the accommodations that are provided appropriately. Eighth, the regulatory mandate regarding confidentiality should be adhered to strenuously.

References

Alexander v. *Choate*, 469 U.S. 287 (83 L. Ed. 2d 661, 1985).

Americans Disabled for Accessible Public Transportation v. *Skinner*, 881 F.2d 1184 (3d Cir. 1989).

Anderson v. *University of Wisconsin*, 665 F. Supp. 1372, aff'd 841 F.2d 737 (7th Cir. 1988).

Arline v. *School Board of Nassau County*, 480 U.S. 273 (1987).

Brennan v. *Stewart*, 834 F.2d. 1248 (5th Cir. 1988).

Carter v. *Bennett*, 840 F.2d 63 (D.C. Cir. 1988).

Doe v. *New York University*, 666 F.2d 761 (2nd Cir. 1981).

Doe v. *Region 13 Mental Retardation Commission*, 704 F.2d 1402 (5th Cir. 1983).

Doe v. *Washington University*, E.D. Mo. (October 2, 1991).

Doherty v. *Southern School of Optometry*, 862 F.2d 570 (6th Cir. 1988).

Harris v. *Thigpen*, 941 F.2d 1495 (11th Cir. 1991).

James v. *Frank*, 772 F. Supp. 984 (S.D. Ohio 1991).

Lau v. *Nichol*, 414 U.S. 563 (1974).

Nathanson v. *Medical College of Pennsylvania*, 926 F.2d 1368 (3d Cir. 1991).

Pandayides v. *Virginia Board of Education*, 752 F. Supp. 696 (E.D. Va. 1990).

Pushkin v. *Regents of the University of Colorado*, 658 F.2d 1372 (10th Cir. 1981).

Rhone v. *United States Department of Army*, 665 F. Supp. 734 (E.D. Mo. 1987).

Salvador v. *Bell*, 622 F. Supp. 438, N.D. Ill. 1985, off'd 800 F.2d 97 (7th Cir. 1986).

Southeastern Community College v. *Davis*, 442 U.S. 397 (1979).

Sweezy v. *New Hampshire*, 354 U.S. 234 (1957).

United States of America v. *Board of Trustees for the University of Alabama*, 908 F.2d 740 (11th Cir. 1990).

Wynne v. *Tufts University School of Medicine*, 932 F.2d 19 (1st Cir. 1991). *Wynne* v. *Tufts University School of Medicine*, WL. 46077 (D. Mass. 1992).

SALOME M. HEYWARD, *a lawyer, is president of Heyward, Lawton and Associates, a firm providing educational institutions and state agencies with consulting services on disability discrimination law issues, and author of* Access to Education for the Disabled *(McFarland, 1992).*

The period between the end of high school and the beginning of college is dynamic for any student. Postsecondary institutions need to consider an array of opportunities as they develop transition programs for undergraduate students of traditional age with disabilities.

Transition to Higher Education

Rhona C. Hartman

For students of traditional age with disabilities, the movement from high school to adult life—movement that can include job entry, admission to postsecondary education or training, and managing a meaningful and satisfying independent life-style—has been termed *transition* by parents, professionals, and recent legislation.

The Individuals with Disabilities Education Act (IDEA) of 1990 (P.L. 101–476) defines *transition services* as a coordinated set of activities for a student, designed within an outcome-oriented process, that promotes movement from school to other activities, which can include postsecondary education, vocational training, integrated employment (including supported employment), continuing and adult education, adult services, independent living, or community instruction.

Many think of transition as a bridge whose size, span, strength, beauty, efficiency, and direction depend on the individual who travels it. This bridge concept differs sharply from the image of door, gateway, or staircase that countless graduation speakers have used to describe the completion of high school. The door image emphasizes abrupt change. The bridge image construes the transition between high school and life after as a system involving feeder lanes, toll gates, and service stations both before and after the bridge itself. This chapter explores that complex system.

Legislative Impetus

The people of the United States have made a major commitment to the education of children and youth with disabilities through high school and beyond. This commitment has been evolving since the mid 1960s, when parents and professionals were instrumental in urging Congress to enact legislation and appropriate money to enable children and youth with disabilities to receive a free appropriate public education. In the 1960s, the Elementary and Secondary Education Act and subsequent amendments laid the groundwork for the landmark P.L. 94–142, the Education for All Handicapped Children Act (EHA) of 1975. The EHA established a core of federal funding for special education, which included money given to the states to provide all children with education and related services in the least-restrictive environment, to ensure due process, and to mandate individualized education plans (IEPs). Parallel with this legislation, Congress also made discretionary funds available. Educational entities compete for these funds in order to test or demonstrate new ideas. Often, the projects supported with these discretionary funds influence future legislation.

Of course, legislation does not happen in a vacuum. It results from citizen activism and political wisdom. The children with disabilities who began school in the 1970s after special education and related services had been mandated were ready to leave the public schools twelve to fifteen years later. They left either by graduating with a high school diploma or certificate, aging out (that is, reaching the age beyond which public schools are not required to serve them), or dropping out. By the early 1980s, many parents and professionals had realized that students who were leaving high school but who were not prepared to enter the work force had few options. Some students with disabilities who appeared academically able to pursue postsecondary education found they had not been counseled accurately and that they were not prepared to succeed in college. College disability support service professionals identified three key problems for entering students with disabilities: inability to articulate disability-related needs; underdeveloped math, science, and language skills; and inexperience in meeting the academic standards expected of college students.

Over the years, amendments to the EHA have refined special education in order to address some of the transition issues. In 1983, amendments extended discretionary programs aimed at facilitating the transition from school to work, established parent training and information centers, and set up the National Clearinghouse on Postsecondary Education for Individuals with Disabilities. By 1986, amendments had established services for preschoolers and expanded transition programs. The 1990 amendments changed the name of the law to the Individuals with Disabilities Education Act (IDEA), expanded the discretionary programs, mandated the inclusion of transition services and assistive technology in IEPs, and extended the categories of disabilities that could be served under the act. According to the thirteenth annual report to Congress on implementation of the Education of the Handicapped Act (U.S. Department of Education, 1991), these refinements helped to increase the proportion of special education students in the nation's elementary and secondary schools to approximately 10 percent of total enrollment.

The fact that increasing numbers of students with disabilities were being educated greatly expanded the options for education after high school.

During the same period, Congress passed several pieces of civil rights legislation that also had an impact on the transition of youth with disabilities from high school to college. The Rehabilitation Act of 1973 and the regulations implementing Section 504 in 1977 played a significant role in enabling students with disabilities to pursue higher education. The Americans with Disabilities Act of 1990 reaffirmed Section 504 and extended the prohibition against discrimination based solely on disability to entities that did not receive federal funds, including those financed by state and local governments and private entities that provide public accommodations. The importance of this legislation for the transition of youth with disabilities to college cannot be overemphasized. Without the civil rights legislation, it is doubtful that colleges and universities would have been as quick as they were to invest resources in making their programs and facilities accessible to students with disabilities.

Activity in the States

Before federal legislation mandated transition planning, parents and professionals in some states responded to the lack of opportunities after high school for students with disabilities by taking the initiative and experimenting with a variety of policies and programs. Often a state-level interagency task force studied the needs and negotiated the agreements necessary for movement from formal, mandated special education to the informal and multidimensional adult world of employment, higher education, and independent living.

By 1992, most of the nation's fifty states had passed legislation on transition services for students between the ages of sixteen and twenty-one. The state initiatives have adopted either an interagency cooperative agreement or a memorandum of understanding (MOU) model to formalize the respective responsibilities of cooperating agencies to provide services that prepare special education students for life after high school. The cooperative agreement or the MOU is usually drawn up between such agencies as the state department of education (usually the lead agency) and departments of vocational rehabilitation and mental health, disability-specific organizations, and perhaps the community college or community college system. For students preparing for college, the state higher education system may be included.

Now that the IDEA has mandated transition planning to begin at the latest by a student's sixteenth birthday, counselors or special education teachers develop a transition plan for each student that is incorporated into the student's IEP or individualized transition plan (ITP). For the student planning to attend college, it is essential for the IEP or ITP to include appropriate academic course work in high school, identify ways for the student to learn self-advocacy skills, and provide some opportunities for extracurricular activities.

•   Many locations also have a statewide system in place to facilitate transition planning for students with disabilities who will be leaving high school. The systems may sound cumbersome on paper, but the fact that most states now have them indicates that the need for options after high school for all students has been recognized. However, in many localities the problem is not that there are few or no programs for students to enter after high school. For students with disabilities graduating from high school and entering college, the programs are there. Instead, the problem is one of raising the aspirations of students, families, and high school faculty.

Model Transition Programs

The HEATH Resource Center, a program of the American Council on Education in Washington D.C., is also the National Clearinghouse on Postsecondary Education for Individuals with Disabilities. Funded since 1984 with discretionary funds from the U.S. Department of Education, it collects and disseminates information about education after high school for students with disabilities. Over the decade of HEATH's operation, numerous materials on transition to college have been developed and disseminated to students with disabilities, their parents, and the professionals who work with them. In addition, HEATH has provided colleges and universities with technical assistance on making programs accessible to students with disabilities. HEATH staff are available by telephone to discuss issues or concerns. A toll-free number makes telephone consultation accessible to consumers and staff at high schools and community colleges. HEATH has a long history of working with the Association of Higher Education and Disability (AHEAD)—the former Association on Handicapped Student Service Programs in Postsecondary Education (AHSSPPE)—a professional organization of disability support service personnel, on numerous joint publications and other projects. Similarly, HEATH has developed and works to maintain an extensive network with organizations of counselors, rehabilitation officials, special educators, and other clearinghouses involved in transition issues. HEATH staff have presented sessions at numerous conferences of network contacts.

The remainder of this section looks at some examples from HEATH files of school-to-college transition programs developed with discretionary funding from the U.S. Department of Education to serve as models of postsecondary education for students with disabilities. The earliest model postsecondary programs, developed between 1975 and the early 1980s, focused on service delivery to students on campus. Such institutions as San Diego Mesa College (California), Western Oregon State College, Southern Illinois University at Carbondale, State University of New York at Buffalo, University of North Dakota, and Wright State University (Ohio) were among the institutions that led the development of systems for students with disabilities (Anderson, Hartman, and Redden, 1981). Other campus programs were developed at this time with funds from other federal sources, including TRIO Student Support Services, or with state funds. The disability support service programs at Ball State University (Indiana), Ohio State University, the University of California at Berkeley, Arizona State University, Pennsylvania State University, Hofstra University and Adelphi University (New York), and Curry College (Massachusetts) were all established in the 1970s. With the interest in transition that developed in the 1980s, the U.S. Department of Education placed priority on this issue in its awards of discretionary funds to postsecondary programs for students with disabilities. The numbers of students with learning disabilities entering college began to increase during this period, and some model transition programs focused on assisting the members of this particular group. The programs described here are examples of such programs.

Pre-College Assessment Program (PCAP), Wright State University. The Pre-College Assessment Program (PCAP) at Wright State University in Dayton, Ohio, gave students with a disability (usually severe) an intensive one-week opportunity to experience college and identify the physical, academic, and self-management skills that they needed in order to succeed. PCAP brought approximately five high school students with disabilities to the college campus each week to analyze their strengths and weaknesses in the skills needed for success in college and to identify the types of colleges to which they might apply. Using a "job analysis" of the college student's role, PCAP staff worked with each student to traverse the campus; use the library, science lab, residence hall, and cafeteria; take notes; write a brief paper; and take part in other college activities. After the five-day session, PCAP staff produced an extensive written and oral report for the student, which was shared with the parent and often with the vocational rehabilitation counselor who had sponsored the student's participation in the PCAP. Results might encourage a student to practice or learn independent living skills before entering college or to select a postsecondary institution that could be counted on to provide specific services. According to the project's final report, students who had been evaluated by PCAP were more likely than others to make a good match when they selected a college and to make a better adjustment once they were there. While PCAP is no longer providing this service, the extensive documentation necessary to replicate it is available through the HEATH Resource Center.

St. Paul Technical College. St. Paul Technical College in St. Paul, Minnesota, has a three-month preparatory program for students who are deaf or hard of hearing and who want to go to college. Participating students, who can come from anywhere in the country, receive training in social skills, independent living, job preparation, and academic and study skills that will help them in college. The program is offered each quarter in the academic year, and students are accepted at any time during the year. Students then enter one of the nation's specialized postsecondary programs for deaf students, such as St. Paul Technical College, the National Technical Institute for the Deaf, or Gallaudet University (Spiers, 1992).

University of North Carolina at Charlotte, Central Piedmont Community College, York Technical College. Together with surrounding school districts, the University of North Carolina at Charlotte, Central Piedmont Community College in Charlotte, North Carolina, and York Technical College in Rock Hill, South Carolina, have created a unique consortium that is designed to identify high school students with learning disabilities and offer them services necessary to select and succeed in one of the consortium's participating institutions. The program has identified a number of strategies that help to enhance the success rate of students with learning disabilities: early identification of students with college potential; provision during the year and at summer precollege programs of intensive tutoring and counseling, especially in self-advocacy skills; and materials developed by the project for use as texts in the activities just described. The program organizes workshops helping students in high school to develop study and social skills and workshops on campus for faculty to increase awareness and help them develop appropriate materials and course modifications. Another interesting feature of the program is that peer mentors selected from among the college students with learning disabilities are paired with high school students to promote self-awareness. The project also works with special educators and counselors in participating high schools to inform them about students' options after high school.

Human Resource Center. The Human Resource Center in Albertson, New York, has developed a number of transition programs for young adults with learning disabilities. The center, which is part of a large rehabilitation facility for individuals with disabilities, works with local high schools, vocational rehabilitation agencies, and four community colleges. Parts of one program, which is designed to promote vocational success for college students, are held at individual high schools to help teachers with the use of appropriate auxiliary aids and teaching strategies. At other times, students go to the Human Resource Center for programs. Parents and the offices of disability support services at the nearby colleges that students will be attending are also involved. A project advisory council with representatives of the groups just named meets regularly to refine project activities, which have included prevocational support, placement readiness, and placement follow-up.

Self-Advocacy Training Projects. The newest types of transition projects to be funded by the U.S. Department of Education are self-advocacy projects. One of the greatest difficulties that students with disabilities have when they leave high school (where they are identified and served) for college (where they are responsible for identifying themselves as having a disability and for requesting necessary services or auxiliary aids) is articulating the barriers. Twelve self-advocacy projects are currently funded to develop curricula, activity guides, and related materials that can teach young high school students with disabilities how to advocate for themselves and how to make changes in the environment.

Self-advocacy training has become instrumental in shaping the provision of campus transition and disability support services across the country. Today, self-advocacy programs exist in every state, in most community colleges, and in private institutions of higher education throughout the United States. The infusion of federal funds in the twelve programs just described should make such training available to increasing numbers of students before they arrive on campus.

Transition Results: A Look at the Data

For many years, students with disabilities have been attending postsecondary institutions, but until recently, the numbers of such students were very small. Not until federal legislation mandated that higher education should be made available to students who are deaf—this legislation created what is now Gallaudet University—were many deaf students educated beyond high school. Similarly, although several programs for disabled war veterans were begun after World War II, it was not until regulations implementing Section 504 of the Rehabilitation Act of 1973 were promulgated in 1977 that the campus landscape began to include students with disabilities in any significant numbers. ·

The national data about students with disabilities are scarce. This section examines three types of data, which indicate that the numbers of students with disabilities are increasing, that students with disabilities now constitute a significant minority on campus, and that the spectrum of disabilities represented on campus has broadened since data were first collected in 1978. This section also reviews high school exit data about students receiving special education and related services to determine the proportion of such students that pursues postsecondary education.

The percentage of full-time freshmen reporting a disability grew dramatically between 1978 and 1991. Almost one in every eleven freshmen (8.8 percent) enrolled in college in 1991 reported having a disability, a considerable change since 1978, when the proportion was one in thirty-eight (2.6 percent). These data (Henderson, 1992), which are based on annual surveys of freshmen by the Cooperative Educational Research Program, which publishes the *American Freshman: National Norms,* are the only national longitudinal data available on college students with disabilities. In 1991, about 140,000 freshmen reported having a disability. While the threefold growth over thirteen years is noteworthy, many believe that the percentages underreport the actual number of students with disabilities, because the survey does not include part-time or returning students, many of whom have disabilities.

If we look instead at the kinds of disabilities that freshmen report, the percentage of disabilities reported that has grown the fastest since 1985 is learning disabilities, which increased from about 15 percent to 25 percent of all disabled students. Freshmen most often report sight and learning disabilities. In 1978, freshmen most often reported sight, orthopedic, and hearing disabilities (President's Committee on Employment of the Handicapped, 1978). Thus, the array of disabilities reported has also changed over time.

Among students enrolled at all levels in the nation's postsecondary institutions, 1.3 million (10.5 percent) reported having at least one disability (Greene and Zimbler, 1989). This figure cannot be compared with figures from the freshmen survey, nor can we make a statement about growth or decline in numbers, because it comes from a survey that was done only once. Nevertheless, the fact that more than 10 percent of the nation's postsecondary students reported having a disability indicates that students with disabilities were a significant minority by the mid 1980s. The kinds of disabilities most often reported among all students, including those in graduate and professional schools, are visual handicaps (40 percent), auditory impairment or deafness (26 percent), and health impairment (25 percent). While there are no data on the retention or graduation of students with disabilities, Greene and Zimbler (1989) report that 8.4 percent of the graduate students and 7.3 percent of the first-year professional students surveyed stated that they had a disability, which indicates that a significant number of the undergraduates with disabilities completed college.

Administrators need to be aware that most students who report anonymously on a survey that they have a disability do not necessarily request service or accommodation or identify themselves on campus as having a disability. Campus disability support service staff report that between 1 and 3 percent of all students on campus request such services. Some request services one year and not the next.

There are no data on the number of college students with disabilities who received special education and related services in high school. We know anecdotally that some college students who request disability support services were either not identified in high school or became disabled after high school—either before enrolling in college or while they were there. Nevertheless, it is instructive to look at high school exit data to see the numbers of students with various disabilities who graduate with a high school diploma or certificate, because they are the most likely to consider a college education.

Of the 220,000 students with disabilities who left the special education system in 1990, fewer than half (44.8 percent) graduated with a diploma. Approximately one-quarter (27.0 percent) dropped out before earning a diploma or certificate. Almost one-eighth (12.4 percent) earned a certificate but not a diploma, and 2.5 percent reached the maximum age served by the public school system. The basis for leaving was unknown for 13.3 percent. These data were reported to the U.S. Department of Education by state education agencies (U.S. Department of Education, 1992).

Students with learning disabilities represent the largest number (129,000) of high school students who left the special education system. More than half (52 percent) earned a diploma. The large number of high school graduates with learning disabilities is consistent with reports from campuses and the freshmen data cited earlier. The other disability groups were much smaller, but their members earned a greater percentage of the diplomas.

Implications for Campus Student Services Staff

How can campus student services staff use information about transition from high school to college to become more effective in their work with all students?

Because in the context of students with disabilities the term *transition* includes the bridge concept, which implies feeder roads and toll gates, the issue of reaching out to high schools and working with secondary administrators, counselors, and special and regular teachers is important. Recruitment and admissions staff and financial aid administrators, who in a sense operate the toll gates, also have much to learn. Deans of students and those who report to them can monitor and help students navigate from the bridge exit ramps onto the main highway, facilitating a safe journey to the student's next transition to graduate school, professional school, or career.

Student services staff, especially recruiters, admissions counselors, and directors of disability support services, can play a key role in bringing the message to secondary school administrators, counselors, and special and regular education teachers that they need to initiate and implement college preparation for students with disabilities. In addition to the services already in place for students who are not disabled, such as college advising, financial aid information, and work sessions about college choice, students with disabilities may need specialized counseling and instruction. It is not too soon to begin considering college plans in junior high school.

Administrators. Postsecondary student services staff can ask junior high and high school administrators certain questions in order to facilitate proactive thinking about transition: Do the secondary schools have systems in place to alert students and parents to the courses that are important for college preparation? If math, science, foreign language, and English literature are necessary for college entrance and success in college, has the administrator made it clear that physical access permits students with disabilities to participate in science education? Has the administrator made it clear that reasonable accommodations and necessary auxiliary aids will be made available so students with disabilities can at least try to succeed in all the college preparatory courses? Has the administrator encouraged counselors, special education teachers, and regular teachers of all subjects to become familiar with the options after high school and with the support services that exist for students with disabilities? If helping teachers to develop such a familiarity entails releasing teachers and counselors for in-service training or collaborating with college counterparts, has the administrator made it a priority to encourage attendance? Has a school staff person been designated to be the liaison with the college admission testing agencies to facilitate an accessible administration of the SAT or the ACT if one is necessary? Are the counselors aware of the many options now open in higher education to students with disabilities? Have they made the extra effort that it might take to raise the awareness of parents and students about the possibilities and to encourage them to prepare for college, if that seems to be the choice? Are students with disabilities encouraged to participate in college fairs? Have counselors and special educators arranged a program for students and parents highlighting the options for students with disabilities? Nearby college disability support service staff are usually eager to assist. Do teachers expect students with disabilities to meet the same academic standards as all students?

(Lowering standards because of disability is a disservice to students, but permitting necessary accommodations or different ways of demonstrating subject mastery is fair. Understanding the difference between lowering standards and making appropriate accommodations is the difference between raising unrealistic expectations and encouraging students to pursue higher education.) Are special education teachers and regular teachers taking the time and making the effort to include a strong self-advocacy program in the curriculum for students with disabilities? Self-advocacy means that the student understands his or her disability, is as aware of the strengths as of the weaknesses resulting from the functional limitation imposed by the disability, and is able to articulate reasonable needs for academic or physical accommodations. Developing self-advocacy takes training and practice. A number of new curricular materials are being developed as a result of federal funding. Are school personnel aware of how to obtain these materials and put them into practice?

Campus Recruitment, Admissions, and Financial Aid Staff. Campus recruitment, admissions, and financial aid staff are the gatekeepers. It is essential for them to become as familiar with the rights of students as they are with the institution's responsibilities toward students with disabilities. Numerous publications are available from HEATH and the relevant professional associations that describe nondiscriminatory procedures for carrying out their functions. To facilitate the transition for students with disabilities, there is much to consider: Have recruitment staff met with campus disability staff to learn firsthand about the services and equipment that are available before going out on the road? Are brochures on campus disability services handed out at college fairs? Does the "viewbook" or other recruiting literature contain photographs of students with a recognizable disability? Such images signal that students with disabilities are welcome on campus and that they are a regular part of campus life. When a recruiter presents a program at a high school, does he or she mention to the general audience, perhaps when he or she discusses the diversity of the student body, that the college has a number of students with disabilities and supply one or two examples that show how those students are doing? Do the packets mailed to prospective students contain information about the disability services office? Are recruitment information and admissions forms available in alternative formats for people who cannot read regular print? (A computer disk or audiocassette of the material would serve this purpose.)

Have college admissions staff reviewed the admissions form to be sure that it does not ask if the applicant has a disability? (It is illegal to do so.) For selective admissions, does the campus have a system in place that allows disability service staff to review and make recommendations about a student whose application does refer to disability? If admissions interviews are expected or available, are they held in accessible places, and can an interpreter be made available if one is requested at the time when the interview is scheduled? Rather than relying solely on standardized test scores and grade point averages, do admissions staff consider a variety of criteria when making decisions? When the offer of admissions is sent, does the packet include an information brochure on disability services? The packet could also include a card that could be returned to inform the disability services office about disability-related access.

Is the financial aid office accessible? Have financial aid administrators informed themselves fully about nondiscriminatory practices in the award of financial aid? Do they have information about disability-specific scholarships? Although the usual practice may be to award aid in a package combining grant, loan, and work-study, disability may prevent some students from working the requisite number of hours, so their package may need to be modified accordingly. Similarly, some students may not be able to take what the institution usually defines as a full-time program. In some cases, the financial aid administrator has the discretion to make the award anyway. Disability-related expenses are a legitimate part of the student's budget. Has the financial aid award taken this into account?

Reaching out to students with disabilities and their parents is another important role for student services staff. Virtually all the questions just asked can be asked of students and parents to raise their awareness of the options. In addition, student services staff can help parents understand their changing role in the advocacy process for their sons and daughters. While the K–12 system expects parents to advocate for their children, the student must be his or her own advocate after high school. Once in a college or university, the student must initiate any request for accommodation and usually provide documentation of the disability. The postsecondary institution has no right or responsibility to identify students in need of services. Also, privacy laws preclude discussion of the student's academic program or progress with parents unless the student has signed a release.

Student services staff can also help parents and students to understand the importance of a good match between student and college. In most cases, students have little choice about the high school that they attend, but for many the choice among the nation's three thousand colleges and universities presents a challenge. Numerous college-choice publications are available, but student services staff can speak from experience by noting that students who have succeeded in a highly structured high school program probably need a similar program on the next level. Those who participated in regular high school, college-preparation classes, and extracurricular activities and who have become articulate self-advocates can probably succeed in larger, more impersonal settings.

Finally, as formalized statewide transition planning initiatives develop, student services staff might be excellent candidates for membership on task forces promoting interagency cooperation and for participation in the development of expanded IEP guidelines for students in transition from high school to postsecondary education.

Orientation and New Student Programs. Student services staff who plan and facilitate the orientation of new students to college have a unique opportunity to smooth the transition for students with disabilities. The goal of any student orientation is to introduce new students to the full spectrum of the life that they will lead on campus so that they will be aware of their rights and responsibilities as members of the college community and able to participate fully. Whether the orientation is for young freshmen new to the college experience, for transfer students, or for older students returning to school, most campuses have put a great deal of thought into orientation activities. First and foremost, are the orientation activities that have been planned for all students accessible for students with disabilities? Is printed information available in alternate format? Since many students hesitate to disclose their disability—indeed, they may not do so until academic problems appear—the regular orientation program is likely to include some people with disabilities. Providing notice during orientation about the support services and accommodations that are available is recommended. Consultation with disability support services staff on the planning of student orientation is important.

Campuses that have a number of students who have identified themselves as disabled after admission but before orientation may consider organizing some orientation activities specifically for students with disabilities. On some campuses, the disability support services officer, working with orientation planners, selects several upper-level students with disabilities to plan these activities and perhaps to act as buddies or mentors for the new students. The activities planned for orientation of students with disabilities could include self-advocacy skills training, locating specialized disability-specific equipment (braille or voice output computers, telecommunications devices for the deaf (TDDs), recorded messages, optical scanning reading machines, braille materials, magnifying equipment, sound amplifiers, and adapted physical education, art, science, and other facilities) on campus, training in the use of such equipment, locating accessible building entrances that students in wheelchairs will need to use, introducing campus security personnel and giving students opportunities to air disability-specific concerns, and introducing key staff with whom particular students will interact. The student with a disability is usually expected to participate in regular orientation as well as in any orientation planned for students with disabilities.

Conclusion

Smooth and successful transition between high school and college for students with disabilities depends on early planning with the student, active training and instruction about options and self-advocacy, open and fair recruiting and admissions policies and procedures, and a full array of student service programs planned and implemented with information about disability and student input. Campuses on which student services staff are informed, accepting, and experienced about serving all students, including students with disabilities, are places where students succeed and move on to other adult pursuits.

References

Anderson, W. R., Hartman, R. C., and Redden, M. R. *Federally Funded Programs for Disabled Students: Models for Postsecondary Campuses.* Washington, D.C.: HEATH/Closer Look Resource Center, American Council on Education, 1981.

Day, E. L., Astin, A. W., Korn, W. S., and Wiggin, E. R. *American Freshman: National Norms.* Washington, D.C.: CERP, American Council on Education, 1992.

Greene, B., and Zimbler, L. *Profile of Handicapped Students in Postsecondary Education, 1987: 1987 National Postsecondary Student Aid Study.* Washington, D.C.: National Center for Education Statistics, Office of Educational Research and Improvement, U.S. Department of Education, 1989.

Henderson, C. *College Freshmen with Disabilities: A Statistical Profile.* Washington, D.C.: HEATH Resource Center, American Council on Education, 1992.

President's Committee on Employment of the Handicapped. *The Disabled College Freshman.* Washington, D.C.: Committee on Employment of the Handicapped, 1978.

Spiers, E. (ed.). *Transition Resource Guide.* Washington, D.C.: HEATH Resource Center, American Council on Education, 1992.

U.S. Department of Education. *To Assure the Free Appropriate Public Education of All Children with Disabilities: Thirteenth Annual Report to Congress on the Implementation of the Individuals with Disabilities Education Act.* Washington, D.C.: U.S. Government Printing Office, 1991.

U.S. Department of Education. *To Assure the Free Appropriate Public Education of All Children with Disabilities: Fourteenth Annual Report to Congress on the Implementation of the Individuals with Disabilities Education Act.* Washington, D.C.: U.S. Government Printing Office, 1992.

RHONA C. HARTMAN is director of the HEATH Resource Center, a program of the American Council on Education located in Washington, D.C. HEATH is the national clearinghouse on postsecondary education for individuals with disabilities.

By capitalizing on the strengths of our past and being open to innovation, student affairs staff can create environments that invite, involve, and retain students with disabilities.

Creating Positive Outcomes for Students with Disabilities

Kevin J. Nutter, Larry J. Ringgenberg

The changing population in higher education has challenged colleges and universities to create learning environments appropriate for an expanding array of individual students. Increasing numbers of part-time, older, international, culturally diverse, and disabled students have irreversibly changed the makeup of our student body.

In 1978, according to the Cooperative Institutional Research Project's (CIRP) survey *American Freshman: National Norms* (Astin, 1978), 2.6 percent of the incoming students reported having a disability. By 1991, that figure had more than tripled, with 8.8 percent identifying themselves as having a disability (Henderson, 1992). The changing mix of these new students requires postsecondary institutions to continue to adjust and accommodate. Kalivoda and Higbee (1989) note that institutions respond to each "new" group of students that arrives on campus by developing policies and practices aimed at accommodating their differences. According to these authors, somewhat less attention has been paid to meeting the highly individualized needs of the newest group, students with disabilities.

As increasing numbers of students with disabilities access campus learning environments, institutions are being challenged to move beyond physical access and provide learning opportunities that are as attitudinally as they are physically conducive to student development. Cheatham (1991) asserts that it is essential for higher education to embrace the task of creating a pluralistic setting that supports an environment in which all students are welcome, regardless of race, ethnicity, socioeconomic background, sexual orientation, or disability. Individuals with disabilities face many of the economic, attitudinal, and institutional obstacles that other "new" students on campus have faced.

NEW DIRECTIONS FOR STUDENT SERVICES, no. 64, Winter 1993 © Jossey-Bass Publishers

Higher education has adapted throughout the years in order to welcome new student constituencies. Attention to new students lies in the ongoing implementation of the *Student Personnel Point of View* (1937, 1949, 1987). The basic concepts expressed in this document have been proven useful as each new group of students has entered higher education. In essence this document views the goals for a college education as promoting the growth of the whole student, including intellectual development in the classroom as well as social-personal development outside the classroom. This perspective also applies to currently enrolled disabled students and to those who will enter as a result of the Americans with Disabilities Act (ADA). Treating each student as an individual and emphasizing the whole person are two important tenets of the ADA.

One focus of the agenda for student affairs is providing an alternative to the impersonalization that characterizes the college experience. Such an alternative can be assured by creating social, physical, and organizational environments that allow the individual to grow and develop (Lyons, 1990).

Traditionally, each new group that has entered higher education has been accompanied by a new group of student affairs practitioners charged with helping to meet their needs. This chapter looks at the literature on retention, ecosystems theory, and new roles for student affairs, including the roles that student affairs must play if students with disabilities are to be integrated and involved in the university environment.

Value-Added Outcomes in Higher Education

Concern with the assessment of student outcomes and the impact of college on students rose sharply during the late 1970s and continued to rise as higher education entered the 1990s (Ewell, 1985a; Pascarella and Terenzini, 1991). A number of factors contributed to this increased attention to the measurement and study of educational impact and outcomes. State and system offices have mandated studies to quantify and explain the benefits of the public investment in higher education, and professional accreditation agencies and organizations are requiring them with increasing frequency.

Central administrators face difficult decisions as resources shrink, and they have turned to outcome data to help ascertain how effectively programs are meeting their intended educational objectives. Concurrently, falling national test scores, the nation's declining educational standing, and continuing high attrition rates have all led the academic quality of our postsecondary institutions to be questioned (NIE Study Group, 1984; Bloom, 1987; Hirsch, 1987).

In addition to the external mandate for increased accountability, college and university administrators are paying more attention to educational impact and outcome data. Such information can be used proactively for a variety of formative purposes, such as evaluation of curricula or examination of the effects of a student support service on student development. Ewell (1985b) observes that a number of national bodies concerned with the quality of postsecondary education have strongly linked outcome assessment with institutional improvement and encourages that evaluative efforts be incorporated into the day-to-day administration of higher education. Student affairs professionals must take an evaluative stance if they hope to provide disabled students with the opportunity and environment to reach their educational goals.

Commenting on the design of effective student services, Huebner (1989) urges the profession first to investigate, then to develop proactive interventions based on research. Reviewing the literature for information on the experiences of students with disabilities, Jane E. Jarrow, executive director of the Association on Higher Education and Disability (AHEAD), observed, "It is important for the reader to keep in mind the newly developed (and developing) nature of the field in order to understand the emphasis on program description and review, rather than data-based research in the literature" (Jarrow, 1987, p. 42). Aune and Kroeger (1993) reached similar conclusions when they sought information on outcome-based investigations of students with disabilities in higher education. Jarrow (1987) notes that student services personnel have been actively involved in the building and expansion of service provision, not in evaluation of the service provided.

"The single largest group of data-based studies of students with disabilities in higher education ha[s] unsuccessfully attempted to differentiate them from their nondisabled peers. In the majority of the studies reviewed and contrary to general hypothesis, students with disabilities are in fact part of the larger population of college students, and their status as disabled has little impact on their attitudes, adjustments, potential, or goals" (Jarrow, 1987, p. 45). Thus, those who want to refine student services for the latest group of "new" students on campus can look to the broader literature for insights on the design of more effective student services.

The growing concern for academic quality and the use of outcome research data to explain, refine, or redesign the educational experience have prompted a number of research approaches to the definition and assessment of educational outcomes. In her interactionist review of the literature on the impact of college and student retention, Stodt (1987) recognized that common factors encourage student persistence, increase the benefits of college, and foster student development. In much the same way, the ecosystems approach (Banning, 1989) to the refinement of educational environments offers a framework for the creation of an educational experience that first invites, then involves, and eventually graduates students with disabilities. Although researchers and theorists have approached retention from a variety of perspectives, several observers have underscored the utility of an interactive perspective for the synthesis and application of the research on student attrition (Noel, Levitz, Saluri, and Associates, 1985; Banning, 1989; Rodgers, 1990; Astin, 1993).

The interactionist or ecosystems perspective states that retention and attrition result from the interactions between students and institutions. We must understand these interactions if we want to understand retention. Characteristics of the interaction, not characteristics only of the student or only of the institution, affect the student's choice to remain or leave the academic setting. The student who remains in school and takes steps to attain his or her educational goals represents a fit between a variety of variables relating to the student and the educational environment, so that leaving school can be viewed as an incongruity between the student and his or her environment. This mismatch, lack of fit, or incongruence between the two can involve a wide array of factors that vary with the individual, the institution, the institution's programs, and the situation. Although the complexity of the factors and interactions does not offer simple explanations, the interactionist view can help us to clarify how students develop and how they can be retained for additional development.

The ecosystems perspective allows us to structure many key retention variables. Beal and Noel (1980) surveyed individuals considered to be most knowledgeable about student retention at 947 two- and four-year institutions. Respondents used a scale ranging from 1 (low) to 5 (high) to rank the importance of a number of positive characteristics for retention. The top four factors that emerged from this survey were caring attitude of faculty and staff (4.29), high-quality teaching (3.90), adequate financial aid (3.69), and student involvement on campus (3.30).

The follow-up study on retention programs conducted by Noel and Levitz (Noel, Levitz, Saluri, and Associates, 1985; Noel and Levitz, 1991) suggests that the research and practice of student affairs continues to support the institutional variables identified more than a decade ago by Beal and Noel (1980).

Tinto (1987) has formulated and refined another perspective on retention that provides a broader sociological conceptualization. He hypothesized that students depart from college when they no longer are socially and academically integrated with others in the educational community and when they no longer share the dominant institutional values. He postulates that student retention or attrition is a by-product of the student's formal and informal academic and cultural interactions with the college and outside communities. This longitudinal process is ongoing and inclusive. Academic and social systems inside and around the college environment interact with the individual student. This model of student retention holds that formal and informal interactions between student and faculty and between student and peers are critical variables.

The quality and the frequency of student and faculty interactions are key factors in efforts to promote students' commitment to the institution and attainment of their educational goals. Outside factors from the larger community also affect a student's commitment to further education. If the student's relationship to the institution and the student's commitment to an educational goal remain firm and if the student values them more than any alternative to college, he or she will remain in the educational environment. If the balance tilts toward an alternative outside the academic setting, a student will leave college. Empirical studies by Pascarella and Terenzini (1980, 1983) support the premises of Tinto's (1987) model and its utility as a framework for understanding and enhancing student retention.

Empirical studies that examine specific individual or institutional characteristics and retention are often limited by their single-setting design. This fact makes it difficult to apply such institutional-specific findings to other settings. One noteworthy exception to this approach can be found in the work of Astin (1978, 1985, 1993). Summarizing his earlier research on retention, Astin (1993) identifies the residential experience and student involvement with peers and with faculty as factors that increase the likelihood that a student will obtain his or her degree. Updating his earlier research, Astin (1993) highlights four other variables that have a positive impact on student retention: previous science preparation, socioeconomic status of student's peers, student orientation of faculty, and humanities orientation of faculty. Three variables have negative effects on retention: institutional size, student employment in a full-time job or part-time off-campus employment, and commuter status.

Astin's (1984) research and observations on the college experience lead him to formulate a theory of student development based on the individual's involvement with the campus environment. The term *involvement* refers to the amount of physical and psychological energy that a student devotes to the educational experience. A student who is highly involved directs considerable energy to such activities as study, social events on campus, participation in student organizations, and interaction with fellow students and faculty. In Astin's view (1984), involvement, as measured by effort and time on task, are critical for the student's learning and development. According to the involvement theory, the student's personal development and learning increase as his or her involvement with the university environment increases.

Longitudinal research conducted by Willingham (1985) surveyed students from nine colleges over a seven-year period. More than 2,300 graduating seniors were asked to identify the factors that did the most and the least to promote a successful and satisfying college experience. More than half of the students polled ranked the following factors as positive: personal contacts with students (89 percent); contacts with faculty and staff (78 percent); time spent on special interests and activities outside class (76 percent); ability to organize tasks and use time effectively (73 percent); work experience during college or in the summer (72 percent); health, attitude, and eating and drinking habits (63 percent); social life on campus (62 percent); sense of direction—knowing why I am in college and what career I would like to work toward (56 percent); and availability of financial resources (52 percent). Successful seniors also identified the last three factors—financial resources (28 percent), sense of direction (23 percent), and social life on campus (23 percent)—as the factors that had kept them from being successful and feeling satisfied with their college experience.

The literature on retention and the ecosystems approach provide the basis for welcoming, involving, and retaining students with disabilities. The litera-ture on retention identifies three essential themes: developing a sense of belonging (transition in); ensuring student involvement in college learning environments (involvement); and clarifying a sense of purpose and direction (transition out). Table 4.1, a matrix of functional goals and anticipated barri-ers, applies these basic themes in an ecosystems framework. Adapted from a cultural diversity training model developed for use in organizations (Sue, 1991), it shows the holistic framework needed for understanding the organi-zational change that is necessary if we are to serve students with disabilities more effectively.

In related work on student development, Schlossberg, Lynch, and Chick-ering (1989) developed a theory of mattering/marginality. This theory states that, if students are to be successful, they must feel that they belong and that people care about them. Students who feel marginal, ignored, and unaccepted are much less likely than others to be successful in the college environment.

Concerted efforts have been made to help students feel less marginal and more involved in the academic experience. Higher education's first attempts in this area were to create service centers for specific groups of students: multi-cultural centers, women's centers, international student centers, and, most recently, disability service offices. The creation of service centers gives students an instant feeling that they matter, because space is perceived as connection with the environment. Physical space also provides a hub for the creation of subcommunities within the college environment.

Lyons (1990) points out that a campus is a collection of small communi-ties. Healthy communities are settings in which students make and keep friends, work together, care about the welfare of others, balance freedom and responsibility, and appreciate human differences. "We are faced with the chal-lenge of creating collegiate communities that are pluralistic yet interactive, where all individuals share a sense of personal and collective worth" (Lyons, 1990, p. 29).

Important Concepts in Student Affairs

To develop an effective student affairs organization, we need a strong belief in the human worth and dignity of others; trust in students, faculty, and other staff; communication between units and among students needing services; flexibility in working with the individual needs of students and staff; and a decentralized, coordinated approach to service delivery.

Human Worth and Dignity. A strong belief in the human worth and dig-nity of others helps us to cherish the differences in people. All students, includ-ing students with disabilities, bring unique characteristics to a college campus. There are different learning styles and different learning timelines, different access needs, and different identity development patterns. An emphasis on human dignity and worth encourages everyone, including students with dis-abilities, to learn about the needs and attributes of others.

Table 4.1. Increased Pluralism and Diversity: A Holistic Approach

Educational Phases	Addressing Obstacles and Barriers to a Pluralistic Environment		
	Intrapersonal Awareness	Interpersonal Differences	Institutional Barriers
Inviting, Recruiting, and Orienting (transition in)	Effectiveness training for disabled and nondisabled individuals	Sensitivity training	Institutional development
		Increased knowledge, communication, teaching, and management skills	Systems intervention
			New policies, programs, and practices
Involvement and Retention (transition through)	Disability awareness and effectiveness training for disabled and nondisabled individuals	Consciousness raising	Institutional development
		Sensitivity training	Systems intervention
		Increased knowledge, communication, teaching, and management skills	New policies, programs, and practices
Academic and Career Planning (transition out)	Disability awareness and effectiveness training for disabled and nondisabled individuals	Consciousness raising	Institutional development
		Sensitivity training	Systems intervention
		Increased knowledge, communication, teaching, and management skills	New policies, programs, and practices

Source: Adapted from Sue (1991)

Trust. Trust continues to be a basic requirement for ensuring that the students in an institution feel valued. Trust means not requiring special permission slips or documentation of a disability. It means providing services that have been requested without concern that it will establish a precedent. And it means having a minimum of rules and regulations to guide student behavior (Lyons, 1990).

Communication. Communication between units and faculty, staff, and students must be complete and precise. One important aspect of communication is listening to one's interlocutor and hearing what he or she is actually saying. Communication is critical when the service delivery model takes the integrated, decentralized approach advocated here. Communication also requires student services to develop ways of hearing from the students whom it serves. Needs assessments are required. Focus groups can be held to discuss issues with students. A conviction to change things that are not working is another requirement for successful communication.

Flexibility. Flexibility is needed when individuals do not fit the traditional model that higher education has developed. Policies on dropping classes, financial aid, residence life, counseling, career services, health centers, and student activities might all need to be adjusted to meet the unique circumstances of disabled students.

Decentralized, Coordinated Approach. Decentralized yet coordinated services are required to help integrate subcommunities of students. Learning takes place in nontraditional forms within student affairs. Learning about individuals is accelerated when all units in a division of student affairs are called on to provide the services needed, including accommodations for disabled students. The decentralized concept can be represented by the loose/tight coupling concept proposed by Peters and Waterman (1982). If we apply this concept to disabled students, we see that the system is loose because a variety of individuals are responsible for creating barrier-free environments, but these individuals are tightly coupled by their strong conviction to the philosophy of equal access. Effective and reliable service in a decentralized system relies on communication. To increase communication capabilities within a decentralized system, each student affairs unit should have a person ensure liaison with disabled student services.

Three-Step Model

Fairweather and Albert (1991) proposed a three-step model for the delivery of services to disabled students that is oriented toward transition. This model, which focuses on helping individuals to move from one environment to another, fits well with the concepts outlined in Table 4.1. The model emphasizes an advocacy role for student affairs staff.

The first step is to identify needs. This needs identification can occur through proactive initiatives with a student's high school or some other agency. This step focuses on finding out about the student instead of waiting for the student to ask for assistance.

The second step is to develop an individualized education program (IEP) for each of the students identified in step one. The focus here is on the individual and on the development of a plan that will work for him or her. A student's IEP can include information about available services, about the university, or both.

After the student enrolls, the service provider actively engages the organization to locate the funds and services that will meet the needs that have been identified. This process can include connecting both with other student affairs units and with academic departments.

Responsibilities of Student Affairs Units

Student affairs organizations can assume certain responsibilities to facilitate the use of their programs and services by disabled students. There are also some general ideas that all units can use to promote a mattering environment that invites, involves, and retains all students, including students with disabilities.

First, analyze the environment. While this analysis includes the physical environment, it should also go beyond architecture. Attention must also be paid to the department's attitudinal environment. Signage and statements of nondiscrimination, posters and artwork that includes people with disabilities should make it clear that disabled students are welcome. Taped materials should be available for individuals with visual impairments. The unit can create an environmental audit team to assess the physical and attitudinal environment for the messages that it sends to disabled students. This assessment should include an analysis of the accessibility of publications and advertisements.

Second, develop liaisons with other offices. Ensure that the staff member charged with liaison is not the only individual who provides services to students with disabilities.

Third, make contact with disabled people. Whenever possible, request staff to utilize other staff and students with disabilities to assist in the delivery of services. Students can benefit from the use of mentors in learning to navigate the campus environment.

Fourth, give all staff in-service training on disability. Use students with disabilities in these sessions. Persons providing services must be knowledgeable about the various aspects of specific disabilities and understand the physical, interpersonal, and institutional barriers facing students on campus (Walker, 1982).

Fifth, monitor the attitudes of program staff, faculty, and the general college community toward students with disabilities and their academic potential.

Student affairs units provide most college students with primary services. While they should also provide disabled students with primary services, the majority of a disabled student's contacts are usually with the disability support services office. Student services units can do a number of things to help create an open and welcoming environment for disabled students: Provide a TDD (Telecommunications Device for the Deaf) telephone number for students with hearing impairments. Provide campus tours in a way that removes access as a problem, that is, by making use of adapted transportation, assistance, or both. Provide and accept application and registration materials and forms in multiple formats (braille, large print, tape). Incorporate interpreters, wheelchair access, and alternative print formats into programs and activities. Provide supplemental orientation addressing matters of particular concern to disabled students, such as access to facilities, programs, services, and activities. Contact prospective disabled students to welcome them to campus and help orient them to their new learning environment. Review all programs, activities, and services to ensure that they are inclusive, accessible, and pluralistic. Provide comparable, convenient, and accessible housing at the same cost as such housing is made available to students who do not have disabilities. Provide recreational activities, including intramural programs that allow disabled individuals to compete. Promote and encourage the development of a disabled student group.

In general, students with disabilities do not need "special" services. They have many of the same developmental and academic concerns as their nondisabled peers, and the members of the two groups share many expectations for their postsecondary academic experience. Nevertheless, two areas in student affairs merit extra emphasis when student affairs works with disabled students: self-disclosure and educational and career planning.

For students with hidden disabilities, such as learning disabilities, psychiatric disabilities, and HIV/AIDS, self-disclosure can involve an agonizing decision. Many of these students have spent most of their lives trying to keep their disability secret. Once in the college setting, they are urged—in fact required—to disclose their disability in order to receive accommodations. This requirement creates a multitude of dilemmas for the student: when to disclose, how to disclose, how much to disclose, to whom to disclose. In essence, the student with a hidden disability makes a decision to "come out," with all the implications of that expression. Student affairs professionals can be instrumental in helping students with this process by being sensitive to the extra burden that disclosure may place on them, explaining why disclosure is necessary and who will have access to the information, assuring students that safeguards have been put into place to ensure confidentiality, and even, if necessary, role-playing appropriate strategies for disclosure.

Educational and career planning presents a challenge because, in contrast to their nondisabled peers, many college students with disabilities begin the career exploration process with no experience of the world of work. Often, they have had few if any opportunities for part-time or volunteer work experience. To compound the problem, older students or severely disabled students who have come from segregated settings may never have had any personal or career development classes. As a result, these students may have debilitatingly low or unrealistically high expectations and career aspirations. For these reasons, the following advice is appropriate for student affairs professionals: Include disability-related information about legal rights under the ADA, disclosure concerns, and job accommodations in career services. To promote self-efficacy, plan activities around career and personal exploration that helps disabled students to value and acknowledge their skills, abilities, and talents. Ensure that students with disabilities are treated as individuals. Each student has different characteristics, strengths, and weaknesses regardless of disability.

Develop employer networks so that students with disabilities can be placed in internships, mentorships, and competitive employment positions. Give students with disabilities opportunities to explore a variety of majors and careers through job shadowing, volunteer work, internships, mentoring, and involvement opportunities. Do not classify certain educational and career paths as appropriate for all people with disabilities. Ensure that students consider a full array of options. Encourage disabled students, but do not enable them. Teach them the skills that they will need in order to develop on their own. Counselors need to encourage, support, and empower students to do for themselves. Finally, when you invite speakers, plan programs, or promote involvement and leadership, make sure that you include role models for persons with disabilities (Aase and Smith, 1992).

Toward a New Partnership

The service delivery models just outlined relate to the process-oriented implementation of total quality management (TQM). Proposed by W. Edwards Deming, TQM recognizes the importance of involving and empowering staff and customers. The 1990s have heard calls for the use of TQM techniques and the philosophy of continuous quality improvement in higher education. The view of student as customer is not foreign to student affairs, and many of the basic tenets of TQM complement the interaction and ecosystems perspective reviewed earlier.

Deming (1986) views an organization as a system. Processes and tasks are linked together and affect one another. A system that wants to excel at meeting the needs of students must be improved (Scholtes, 1992). The system includes everything that a student experiences on the university campus: the physical and social environment, the people, and the policies and procedures in place at the institution. Deming also calls for breaking down barriers between departments (Scholtes, 1992). People within a student affairs division and people within the institution need to work as a team. The barriers created by scarce resources need to be eliminated by a steadfast commitment to a philosophy of care about all individuals. In addition, individuals need a vigorous program of education and self-improvement.

Customer analysis is one of the principal concepts of TQM. The principal customers of higher education are students in all their diversity. However, it has a number of other customers: administrative offices, faculty, community members, prospective students, and parents. The goal is for every office on campus to meet or exceed the expectations of all its customers (Marchese, 1991). The focus on customers has caused staff to stop explaining and start listening to what customers want (Seymour, 1991). "A customer orientation shifts priorities of the institution and its employees from generating policies and rules to generating opportunities to learn about customer expectations and requirements" (Seymour, 1991, p. 10).

Universities are sometimes organized as a series of pigeonholes. Department structures and rigid divisions separate and isolate business, student, and academic affairs. One possible consequence of the resulting disconnectedness is that critical processes can be micromanaged. TQM allows us to understand the entire work process in a comprehensive way. People from different areas can concentrate on commonalities and on processes rather than on differences and personalities (Seymour, 1991).

Barriers have existed between student affairs practitioners and other segments of the campus community during much of the profession's existence. Twenty years ago, partnerships between faculty and student affairs were proposed as one way of breaching these barriers (Brown, 1972). Little progress has been made toward creating such partnerships. TQM should make it possible to remove the barriers between academic affairs and student affairs. Serving various "new" populations, such as disabled students, can serve as a catalyst for this type of activity. The institution needs to start with a vision and a commitment to serve disabled students as a shared responsibility. Coordination can lie within student affairs, but all parts of the institution must share the commitment and willingness to meet the challenges.

Collaborating with faculty is also extremely important in responding to diversity. A broad definition of diversity includes all "new" students. Student affairs staff must provide faculty with support and assistance in understanding the needs of all students, including students with disabilities. The focus and the educational process that results from TQM can help remove existing barriers. Serving new populations and helping faculty to understand these new students will serve as a catalyst for this new collaboration.

Conclusion

This chapter has examined our knowledge of what students need in order to have successful undergraduate experiences, and it has applied that knowledge to students with disabilities. Both disabled and nondisabled students need to make connections and become involved with the institution. Both disabled and nondisabled students need to feel that they matter to the institution. Student affairs staff can demonstrate their concern by being respectful, trusting, and appreciative of differences in their interactions with students. A collaborative relationship between student affairs staff and faculty is essential if all students, including those with disabilities, are to be served.

References

Aase, S., and Smith, S. *A Handbook for Teaching Career Development to Students with Disabilities.* Minneapolis: Disability Services, University of Minnesota, 1992.

Astin, A. W. *American Freshman: National Norms.* Washington, D.C.: American Council on

Education and University of California, Los Angeles, 1978.

Astin, A. W. "Student Involvement: A Developmental Theory for Higher Education." *Journal of College Student Personnel*, 1984, *25*, 297–308.

Astin, A. W. *Achieving Educational Excellence: A Critical Assessment of Priorities and Practices in Higher Education*. San Francisco: Jossey-Bass, 1985.

Astin, A. W. *What Matters in College? Four Critical Years Revisited*. San Francisco: Jossey-Bass, 1993.

Aune, E., and Kroeger, S. *Career Services on College Campuses: Are They Ready for Students with Disabilities?* Minneapolis: Disability Services, University of Minnesota, 1993.

Banning, J. H. "The Campus Ecology Manager Role." In U. Delworth, G. R. Hanson, and Associates, *Student Services: A Handbook for the Profession*. (2nd ed.) San Francisco: Jossey-Bass, 1989.

Beal, P. E., and L. Noel. *What Works in Student Retention*. Iowa City: American College Testing Program, National Center for Higher Education Management Systems, 1980.

Bloom, A. *The Closing of the American Mind*. New York: Simon & Schuster, 1987.

Brown, R. D. *Student Development in Tomorrow's Education: A Return to the Academy*. Washington, D.C.: American College Personnel Association, 1972.

Cheatham, H. E. (ed.). *Cultural Pluralism on Campus*. Alexandria, Va.: American College Personnel Association, 1991.

Ewell, P. "Some Implications for Practice." In P. Ewell (ed.), *Assessing Educational Outcomes*. New Directions for Institutional Research, no. 47. San Francisco: Jossey-Bass, 1985a.

Ewell, P. "The Value-Added Debate . . . Continued." *American Association for Higher Education Bulletin*, 1985b, *38*, 12–13.

Fairweather, J. S., and Albert, J. J. "Organizational and Administrative Implications for Serving Students with Disabilities." In H. E. Cheatham (ed.), *Cultural Pluralism on Campus*. Alexandria, Va.: American College Personnel Association, 1991.

Henderson, C. *College Freshman with Disabilities: A Statistical Profile*. Washington, D.C.: American Council on Education, 1992.

Hirsch, E. *Cultural Literacy: What Every American Needs to Know*. Boston: Houghton Mifflin, 1987.

Huebner, L. "Interaction of Student and Campus." In U. Delworth, G. R. Hanson, and Associates, *Student Services: A Handbook for the Profession*. (2nd ed.) San Francisco: Jossey-Bass, 1989.

Jarrow, J. E. "Integration of Individuals with Disabilities in Higher Education: A Review of the Literature." *Journal of Postsecondary Education and Disability*, 1987, *5*(2), 38–57.

Kalivoda, K. S., and Higbee, J. L. "Students with Disabilities in Higher Education: Redefining Access." *Journal of Educational Opportunity*, 1989, *2*(1), 14–21.

Lyons, J. W. "Examining the Validity of Basic Assumptions and Beliefs." In M. J. Barr, L. A. Keating, and Associates, *New Futures for Student Affairs: Building a Vision for Professional Leadership and Practice*. San Francisco: Jossey-Bass, 1990.

Marchese, T. "TQM Researches the Academy." *AAHE Bulletin*, November 1991, pp. 3–9.

NIE Study Group. *Involvement in Learning: Realizing the Potential of American Higher Education*. Washington, D.C.: National Institute of Education, 1984.

Noel, L., and Levitz, R. (eds.). *Compendium of Successful, Innovative Retention Programs and Practices*. Coralville, Iowa: Centers for Institutional Effectiveness and Innovation, 1991.

Noel, L., Levitz, R., Saluri, D., and Associates. *Increasing Student Retention: Effective Programs and Practices for Reducing the Dropout Rate*. San Francisco: Jossey-Bass, 1985.

Pascarella, E. T., and Terenzini, P. T. "Predicting Freshman Persistence and Voluntary Dropout Decisions from a Theoretical Model." *Journal of Higher Education*, 1980, *51*, 60–75.

Pascarella, E. T., and Terenzini, P. T. "Predicting Voluntary Freshman-Year Persistence/Withdrawal Behavior in a Residential University: A Path-Analytic Validation of Tinto's Model." *Journal of Educational Psychology*, 1983, *75*, 215–226.

Pascarella, E. T., and Terenzini, P. T. *How College Affects Students: Findings and Insights from Twenty Years of Research*. San Francisco: Jossey-Bass, 1991.

Peters, T. J., and Waterman, R. W. *In Search of Excellence: Lessons from America's Best-Run Companies*. New York: Harper and Row, 1982.

Rodgers, R. L. "Recent Theories and Research Underlying Student Development." In D. G. Creamer and others (eds.), *College Student Development: Theory and Practice for the 1990s*. Alexandria, Va.: American College Personnel Association, 1990.

Schlossberg, N. K., Lynch, A., and Chickering, A. W. *Improving Higher Education Environments for Adults: Responsive Programs and Services from Entry to Departure*. San Francisco: Jossey-Bass, 1989.

Scholtes, P. R. *The Team Handbook: How to Use Teams to Improve Quality*. Madison, Wisc.: Joiner Associates, 1992.

Seymour, D. T. "TQM on Campus: What the Pioneers Are Finding." *AAHE Bulletin*, November 1991, pp. 10–18.

Stodt, M. M. "Educational Excellence as a Prescription for Retention." In M. M. Stodt and W. M. Klepper (eds.), *Increasing Retention: Academic and Student Affairs Administrators in Partnership*. New Directions for Higher Education, no. 60. San Francisco: Jossey-Bass, 1987.

Student Personnel Point of View. Washington, D.C.: American Council on Education, 1937.

Student Personnel Point of View. Washington, D.C.: American Council on Education, 1949.

Student Personnel Point of View. Washington, D.C.: American Council on Education, 1987.

Sue, D. W. "A Model for Cultural Diversity Training." *Journal of Counseling and Development*, 1991, 70, 99–105.

Tinto, V. *Leaving College: Rethinking the Causes and Cures of Student Attrition*. Chicago: University of Chicago Press, 1987.

Walker, P. "Programs for Individuals: One Viewpoint on Providing Services to Disabled Students." *Journal of NAWDAC*, 1982, 45(4), 16–21.

Willingham, W. *Success in College: The Role of Personal Qualities and Academic Ability*. New York: College Entrance Examination Board, 1985.

KEVIN J. NUTTER is career services program director, University Counseling and Consulting Services, University of Minnesota–Twin Cities.

LARRY J. RINGGENBERG is director of student activities and centers at the University of Wisconsin–Lacrosse.

Service delivery systems face many challenges in the 1990s. Coordinating key features common to successful programs and building in consistent evaluative practices will enable higher education to achieve full participation by people with disabilities.

Essential Elements in Effective Service Delivery

Judy Schuck, Sue Kroeger

Programs for students with disabilities in higher education were introduced in the early 1970s, and they have grown significantly in scope and sophistication since that time. However, they vary widely in the quality and consistency of the services that they provide. As our knowledge about optimal service provision has increased, so has our awareness of the issues and challenges facing us as we move into the 1990s and full implementation of the Americans with Disabilities Act (ADA). This chapter examines the current state of higher education programs for students with disabilities; defines essential program standards and components and examines related service delivery issues; and makes recommendations for student services professionals who are striving to achieve full participation by people with disabilities in all institutions of higher education.

Diversity Among Institutions

Sandeen (1989) observes that five factors affect the organization of a student affairs division: staff competence, institutional characteristics, student characteristics, institutional resources and facilities, and student affairs division goals. These same factors influence the organization and provision of disability services. As a consequence, programs for students with disabilities vary widely from one institution to the next. Some institutions include access for disabled students in their mission statement, their diversity statement, or both. Others make no mention of such students in any institutional publication or communication. On some campuses, services are directed by a student services professional for whom the role of Section 504 coordinator is only one of his or her many responsibilities. At other institutions, disability services is a unit in its own right, with specialized staff ranging from counselors for specific disability groups (for example, mobility, sensory, learning, psychiatric) to communication access specialists. At some institutions, programs are highly centralized, with most services emanating from and funded by the disabilities services office. At others, services are decentralized, and each unit is expected to respond to the needs of the disabled students who wish to access its programs and activities. At some institutions, disability services is a unit within the student affairs division. At others, the program reports to the chief academic officer. Still other institutions separate services for students with physical disabilities from services for students with learning disabilities and house the two units in different divisions.

Clearly, inconsistent services are a significant problem in higher education's programs for students with disabilities. Services that one can routinely expect on one campus may not be routine on another. And if a service is available at two different institutions, the level of service or the method of delivery can vary dramatically from one institution to the other. Many campuses provide comprehensive services to students with one type of disability and few or no services to students with other types of disabilities (Bonney, 1988).

Nevertheless, passage of the ADA makes it clear that institutions of higher education must examine and if necessary change their disability service programs if they are to ensure access for students with disabilities. To make such examination and change possible, institutions must predicate services for disabled students on clearly stated goals, and these services must have certain common elements as well as a coordinating authority.

Goals for Services

In establishing goals for disability services, it is helpful to keep in mind the *CAS Standards and Guidelines for Student Services/Development Programs,* which were developed in 1986 by the Council for the Advancement of Standards for Student Services/Development Programs (1988) in collaboration with twenty-two professional organizations. In addition to the general standards, which pertain to all areas of student services, CAS also developed standards and guidelines specific to disability programs. The CAS standards and guidelines for disabled student services, an appendix to the *CAS Standards and Guidelines for Student Services/Development Programs* (1988), state that program goals need to reflect an institution's characteristics and the resulting program should

- Advocate responsibly on behalf of the needs of disabled students to the campus community so that nondisabled individuals gain a general awareness of and sensitivity to the circumstances of disabled students
- Assess the needs of disabled students and the campus units with which they interact in meeting those needs

- Coordinate the actions, policies, and procedures of individuals, units, and departments that affect disabled students
- Ensure that disabled students have equal access to all institutional programs and services (CAS, 1986)

Essential Program Elements

The program goals just reviewed cannot be achieved unless certain program elements have been put into place. Eleven elements seem to characterize effective disability services no matter what their size or mode of delivery: outreach, verification and certification of disability, assessment, information and referral, case management, accommodations, support, advocacy, training, consultation, and reporting and evaluation.

Outreach. One of the most significant differences between Section 504 of the Rehabilitation Act of 1973, which regulates services to students with disabilities in higher education, and P.L. 94–142, which governs the provision of special education in the K–12 system, is the way in which individuals access services. P.L. 94–142 requires the school system to seek out and assess students in need of special education. In contrast, Section 504 prohibits institutions from identifying students with disabilities and requires students both to identify themselves as disabled and to initiate the request for services. The Section 504 requirements make outreach, both internal and external, the first fundamental component of a disability services office. Moreover, the ADA makes it increasingly apparent that outreach needs to be conducted in a variety of formats, including print, audiotape, and electronic media.

Verification and Certification of Disability. Both Section 504 regulations and the ADA require individuals to have a verified disability in order to access their rights under the law. In most cases, verification means that students who request accommodations or who wish to use other disability-related programs and services must register with the disability services program or officer and furnish documentation of their disability. The critical issue that this component raises is the issue of confidentiality. Students must understand who will have access to the documentation that they supply. They must be assured that it will not be shared inappropriately with other campus units. Perhaps more than any other area in the institution, disability services must have clear policies and practices regarding data privacy. Privacy is particularly important for hidden disabilities, such as HIV/AIDS and psychiatric disabilities.

Assessment. Once a student has registered with the disability services office, he or she and the environment in which he or she must function must be assessed in order to determine necessary services and accommodations. Some individuals, particularly if they are coming from the K–12 system or if they have been referred by another agency, such as vocational rehabilitation, may submit a comprehensive assessment as part of their verification of disability. Others, particularly older returning adults, may have assessment information that is outdated. If they were not previously identified as having a disability, there may be no assessment data at all.

The absence of assessment data is often a problem for older students who suspect that they have a learning disability but who were never diagnosed as being disabled in this way. When no assessment data are available, a careful intake and screening procedure is essential, and this screening must be accompanied by effective interagency cooperation. Assessment is costly and time-consuming. Only by having extensive knowledge of and positive relationships with community and government agencies that might share the assessment function can the disability services office avoid unnecessary delays and duplication of effort when helping a student to obtain a comprehensive evaluation of his or her abilities and disabilities.

An assessment of the environment in which the student must function is as important as an assessment of the individual. Accommodations that might be necessary for the student in one class or with one instructor might not be necessary elsewhere. For example, a student with a learning disability may need a taped textbook in an economics class that requires heavy reading assignments, but he or she will be able to do the required reading independently in an acting class in which the textbook only supplements class activities. A student with a mobility impairment may require a lab assistant in a chemistry lab but not in a sculpture class. The needs of students with disabilities are diverse. A thorough assessment of the student and his or her environment assures that the institution considers each person as an individual and attends to his or her unique educational needs (Dahlke, 1991).

Information and Referral. Even at large institutions that have extensive resources, it is inappropriate and unrealistic for any single service office to assume the responsibility of providing disabled students with all the programs, services, and activities that the institution offers. In smaller institutions, limited personnel and limited financial assets mean that efforts to provide adequate services for students with disabilities must tap all the resources available both inside and outside the institution (Sheridan and Ammirati, 1991). The information and referral function is another critical element for a viable disability services program, because it helps students navigate the campus and surrounding community. Fulfilling this function means that staff must first conduct an assessment of campus and community resources, then network continually with these resources to help them understand students' needs, elicit their support in meeting students' needs, and keep disability services information current. Dahlke (1991) recommends that the disability office assemble a resource guide identifying the services available on campus; the services available off campus through social service and community agencies; where the services are located, including addresses and telephone numbers; the person or persons who need to be contacted in order to initiate the services; any special fees associated with the services; and any timelines or deadlines that must be observed in order to receive services.

Case Management. Case management is another important program element. Because tightening fiscal constraints and the threat of litigation have placed disability services under increased scrutiny, it is important for them to keep careful and accurate records on the students with whom they deal. These records should include information about verification of disability; permission to release confidential material; contacts with the disability office, faculty, and campus and community offices and agencies; and student contracts. Case management is often neglected, because it is time-consuming and because there are always more immediate problems that need to be solved. Nevertheless, the time spent on good case management, even in small programs, helps the disability services office to defend the efficacy of its programs and to prevent costly duplication of effort and miscommunication between the departments that interface with the student.

Accommodations. Providing reasonable accommodations for students with disabilities is perhaps the most basic function of the disability services office, because accommodations are the key to program accessibility. *Accommodation* has been defined as an adjustment to the learning environment that does not compromise the essential elements of a course or curriculum. Accommodations take a variety of forms: auxiliary aids, such as notetakers and sign language interpreters; assistive technology, such as reading machines and voice-activated computers; texts and other reading material in alternative formats, such as braille, large print, and audiotape; test adaptations, such as extended time and distraction-free testing sites; and policy or program modifications, such as priority registration, reduced credit loads, and second language substitutions.

While many faculty members routinely allow for academic accommodations and in fact offer them to all students, some faculty see them as intrusive, as giving disabled students an unfair advantage, as lowering standards, as interfering with academic freedom, or as imposed on them by an administrator fearful of lawsuits. The student services administrator can play an important role in addressing the concerns of faculty members about reasonable accommodations by stressing that the purpose of such accommodations is to ensure that disabled students have access to programs, not to change criteria or performance levels in ways that will diminish or dilute program standards. The student services professional can also ensure that test security is adequately safeguarded, that the criteria and procedures for accessing accommodations are clearly delineated and disseminated to the entire campus community, and that accommodations are determined with input from all concerned—instructor, student, disability service provider or unit—whenever possible. Nevertheless, in the final analysis the expertise needed to determine whether a given accommodation is suitable rests with the disability services provider. The law entitles students with disabilities to appropriate accommodations.

Individual and Group Support. Like other students, students with disabilities may fail or choose not to persist for reasons other than academic ones.

Indeed, the facts that disabled students experience more pressure to "adjust" to their environment and have fewer opportunities to become involved in it may place them at greater risk of dropping out than other students. Thus, providing individual support, group support, or both, in such forms as counseling, peer support groups, and self-advocacy instruction, is as crucial for the success of students with disabilities as ensuring academic accommodations.

Teaching self-advocacy skills is especially important for students who come to postsecondary education directly from K–12 special education programs or from segregated settings that have not prepared them to negotiate for their own needs, as they must in the postsecondary setting. As noted earlier, Section 504 regulations assign responsibility for initiating requests for service to the student, not the institution. This is a difficult adjustment for students who have never been asked to identify or articulate their own needs (Scales, 1986). In addition to their importance for entering students, self-advocacy skills are also fundamental for making the transition out. Students who have not learned to be their own advocates in an educational setting will no doubt find it difficult to advocate for themselves in the workplace.

Advocacy. Advocating for the rights of students has always been considered a paramount function of student services professionals, and this function is even more important when they deliver disability services.

One of the simplest forms of advocacy is for the disability services officer to be the voice that represents students with disabilities on a daily basis. Because disabled students are a relatively new population on many campuses, staff may not always consider how changes in policies and procedures may affect them. For example, what appears to be a simple scheduling change could mean that a disabled student could no longer use paratransit services. In such cases, advocacy often means simply asking how such a change will affect students with disabilities.

Another form of advocacy is networking, both on campus and in the community. Huss (1982) defines networking as building a core of individuals throughout the university in a systematic and conscious way so persons in strategic areas of the campus are working on behalf of disabled students.

Networking within the community is just as important. More than the members of other groups, disabled students must interact with a myriad of community groups and agencies—vocational rehabilitation, social security, independent living centers, paratransit services, attendant care providers, interpreter referral services, to name just a few. Establishing a close working relationship with such agencies not only makes it possible for disability services to advocate for the individual students who use their services, but it also enables them to form coalitions when programs are threatened, to avoid costly duplication of effort, and to sponsor joint programs.

The defense of programs and services that are already in place is another, more critical form of advocacy. Again, because disability services are relatively new on many campuses, they are often funded with soft money, or they have not been fully institutionalized. Fiscal constraints can make the staff who deliver these services vulnerable to budget cuts—victims of last hired, first fired logic. Disability services, like disabled students, need to be skilled in self-advocacy.

The last form of advocacy that needs to be reviewed here is working on behalf of individual students with faculty members. While disability service providers may wish that students could always negotiate their own accommodations with faculty, they will doubtless encounter an intransigent faculty member who refuses to have a tape recorder in the classroom, protests that an interpreter will be intrusive, or denies extended time on a test because it would be unfair to other students. In such cases, the service provider may have to "invoke the law" and inform the instructor that what the student is requesting is his or her right and therefore not negotiable.

Training. Training is second in importance only to providing students with direct accommodations. Faculty training is first and foremost. For example, a survey of the needs and concerns of disabled students at the University of Arizona found that the majority of respondents in each disability category agreed that a heightened awareness by faculty would make their academic life more successful (Moore, Newlon, and Nye, 1986). As Nathanson (1983, p. 48) states, "faculty attitudes and behaviors toward students who are physically disabled have the potential to enhance and facilitate their integration into the college community or can pose a formidable barrier, which, in a very real sense, can be a greater obstacle than the more commonly considered architectural barriers." While the author just quoted is speaking of students with physical disabilities, his comments are equally if not more relevant to students with hidden disabilities, such as learning or psychiatric disabilities. Not only do these students sometimes encounter insensitive faculty, they may not be believed when they request accommodations owing to the erratic and invisible aspects of their disabilities.

Of course, the need for training is not limited to faculty. As recent self-evaluations for the ADA have indicated, administrators in facilities and communications have as large a role to play in ensuring access as those in student services and academic affairs. Support staff, too, ranging from maintenance people to library staff, are key to ensuring access for disabled students. If staff in all units are trained effectively, they assume their rightful responsibility and opportunity to serve disabled students as they do other students and reduce the need for disability services to devote time to advocacy.

While the importance of training is widely acknowledged, there is as yet little agreement on the kind of training that is most effective. It is generally agreed that opportunities for faculty and staff to interact directly with disabled students are important.

Consultation. Like training, consultation has assumed increasing importance as institutions extend their commitment to access beyond doors and ramps to programs, services, and activities. Again, the ADA self-evaluations make it clear that many campus groups, ranging from faculty and administration in academic and student affairs to personnel from such areas as information services, campus security, and human resources, will look to disability services for advice and expertise as they strive to comply with the new rules and regulations.

Reporting and Evaluation. In the past, most disability service offices focused on developing and ensuring access and placed relatively little emphasis on determining what happens to students as a result of this access. This focus is changing significantly. As mentioned earlier, fiscal constraints can make disability services vulnerable. Funding can be reduced or eliminated. Competition for limited dollars is stiff, and disability programs, like other student services units, are increasingly being challenged to demonstrate that their services and activities are effective. Aside from issues bearing directly on funding, the general movement today within institutions, accrediting bodies, and legislatures is to assess student outcomes in all aspects of higher education. This movement will certainly not bypass disability services, and it provides additional impetus to implement comprehensive evaluation plans.

Little has been written about program evaluation in disability services. Many programs tend to rely primarily on individual "success stories." However, ongoing data collection, which is integral to any evaluation plan, is particularly important for disability services, because funding is often tied to the number of students served. Dahlke (1991) suggests that data are also useful in justifying the need for the program; assessing the effectiveness of the services provided; determining whether students and staff are satisfied with the services; identifying ways in which the program can be improved; and projecting program growth and needed funding increases.

The Need for Coordination

While most professionals in the disabilities field would agree that the components just reviewed are critical to the success of any program, it should be equally apparent that these components cannot be developed or delivered effectively without coordination. Moreover, in the absence of central coordination, the other disability-related services, such as adapted physical education or assistive computer technology, that might be found on a campus in a variety of formats may either duplicate existing efforts or fail to provide access. Coordination also lays the groundwork for communication with students. Making the ADA or Section 504 coordinator or the disability services office known to students and having a single telephone number that students can call for information or at least for referral increase the likelihood that students will locate the services that they need (Fairweather and Albert, 1991).

To ensure this coordination, the institution must make an office or an individual responsible for ensuring access for students with disabilities. Depending on its resources, the institution may want to house this individual or office in an existing program or make it a unit on its own. What is important is not the location of the service coordinator within the institution's administrative structure but, as King (1982) points out, that the service coordinator has the expertise and clear authority to act effectively.

Conclusion

The ADA required all colleges and universities to complete by January 1993 an institutional self-study assessing the accessibility of their programs, services, and activities to students with disabilities. It also required them to begin implementing immediately any needed corrective measures.

Discussion of these self-studies among professionals in the disability field underscores that, if we are to reach our goal of full access for all students with disabilities in higher education, each institution must have an effective disability services office or at least an officer. Disability services must include the essential components discussed in this chapter, and they need to be coordinated by a competent staff person who has a clear and visible line of authority and support from top administration.

Whether or not the disability services office is housed in the student services unit, student services administrators can play a key support role by becoming well informed about the ADA, establishing access as a priority goal in the mission of the institution, infusing access within all other student services divisions, providing ample staff development and training opportunities, and advocating adequate funding for disability services.

References

Bonney, S. Testimony presented on behalf of the Association on Handicapped Student Service Programs in Postsecondary Education (AHSSPPE) to the National Council on the Handicapped, July 1987. In *Capitalizing on the Future, Proceedings of the 1987 AHSSPPE Conference.* Columbus, Ohio: AHSSPPE, 1988.

Council for the Advancement of Standards for Student Services/Development Programs. *CAS Standards and Guidelines for Student Services/Development Programs.* N.p.: Council for the Advancement of Standards for Student Services/Development Programs, 1988.

Dahlke, C. *Support Programs in Higher Education for Student with Disabilities: Access to All.* Gaithersburg, Md.: Aspen Publishers, 1991.

Fairweather, J., and Albert, J. "Organizational and Administrative Implications for Serving College Students with Disabilities." In H. Cheatham and others (eds.), *Cultural Pluralism on Campus.* Alexandria, Va.: ACPA Media Board Publications, 1991.

Huss, J. K. "Strategies for a Decentralized Delivery System." In *Handicapped Student Service Programs in Postsecondary Education: Proceedings of the Fifth National Conference.* Columbus, Ohio: Association on Handicapped Student Service Programs in Postsecondary Education, 1982.

King, W. L. "Student Services' Response to Learning-Disabled Students." In M. R. Schmidt and H. Z. Sprandel (eds.), *Helping the Learning-Disabled Student.* San Francisco: Jossey-Bass, 1982.

Moore, C. J., Newlon, B. J., and Nye, N. "Faculty Awareness of the Needs of Physically Disabled Students in the College Classroom." *AHSSPPE Bulletin,* 1986, 4(4), 136–145.

Nathanson, B. "Attitudes and Behaviors Toward Physically Disabled Students: Discussions with Faculty." *AHSSPPE Bulletin,* 1983, 1(2), 48–60.

Sandeen, A. "Issues Influencing the Organization of Student Affairs." In V. Delworth, G. R. Hanson, and Associates, *Student Services: A Handbook for the Profession.* (2nd ed.) San Francisco: Jossey-Bass, 1989.

Scales, W. "Postsecondary Education for Disabled Students: Written Testimony." *AHSSPPE Bulletin,* 1986, 4(1), 20–32.

Sheridan, M., and Ammirati, T. "A Private College's Response to the Emerging Minority of Students with Disabilities." *Journal of Postsecondary Education and Disability*, 1991, *9*(4), 291–299.

JUDY SCHUCK is associate dean of student services and former director of the office for students with disabilities at Minneapolis Community College, Minneapolis, Minnesota.

SUE KROEGER is director of disability services at the University of Minnesota–Twin Cities.

Postsecondary education has become an option for increasing numbers of individuals with learning disabilities. College personnel must be prepared to provide academic adjustments and accommodations for the members of this growing population.

Students with Learning Disabilities

Lydia S. Block

The percentage of college freshmen with disabilities has tripled since the 1970s (Hartman, 1992). One in four has reported that he or she has a learning disability (Henderson, 1992). The growing population of learning-disabled (LD) students has made it necessary to expand existing services and develop new ones.

This chapter defines *learning disability* and reviews the characteristics of LD students. Next, it addresses a number of topics raised by providing access to LD students, including identification, admissions, and academic accommodations. It concludes with an examination of policy implications for student services personnel and with recommendations for the future.

Definition and Characteristics

The term *learning disability* has been defined in a variety of ways since it was coined in the 1960s (Kirk, 1962). The definition that most subscribe to today is that of the National Joint Committee on Learning Disabilities (NJCLD), which is composed of representatives from national organizations that are interested in or that serve LD individuals. The NJCLD defines *learning disability* as "a general term that refers to a heterogeneous group of disorders manifested by significant difficulties in the acquisition and use of listening, speaking, reading, writing, reasoning, or mathematical abilities. These disorders are intrinsic to the individual, presumed to be due to central nervous system dysfunction, and may occur across the life span. Problems in self-regulatory behaviors, social perception, and social interaction may exist with learning disabilities but do not themselves constitute a learning disability. Although learning disabilities may occur concomitantly with other handicapping conditions (for example, sensory impairment, mental retardation, serious emotional disturbance) or with extrinsic influences, such as cultural differences [and] insufficient or inappropriate instruction, they are not the result of those conditions or influences" (National Joint Committee on Learning Disabilities, 1988).

As the definition notes, LD individuals are a heterogeneous group. It is therefore difficult to make generalizations about the characteristics of LD students (Mangrum and Strichart, 1988). Nevertheless, LD students have a number of characteristics in common.

The literature contains several articles describing the writing skills of LD individuals (Gregg, 1983; Vogel and Moran, 1982; Ganschow, 1984). There are many LD college and university students who have difficulty learning the rules of spelling and grammar, proofreading, expressing themselves adequately in writing, and generally organizing their thoughts on paper.

Much less has been written about the reading skills of this population. Mangrum and Strichart (1988) characterize the reading issues of LD students as difficulty in decoding unfamiliar words, identifying main ideas, maintaining an efficient reading rate, and remembering the material read. Students with reading problems also sometimes see letters out of order and have trouble processing what they read in a meaningful way.

In mathematics, LD students have difficulty working with fractions, decimals, and percentages and in mathematical reasoning. They sometimes also have trouble visualizing, memorizing appropriate sequences, copying numbers correctly, and discriminating between symbols (Mangrum and Strichart, 1988). Difficulty in learning mathematical functions and applying them automatically may be another characteristic of learning disability in mathematics.

LD students often have inadequate organizational and study skills. They have difficulty locating and organizing the materials needed in order to study, allocating sufficient time for study, finding the right environment in which to study, making and adhering to schedules, and identifying the points that they need to study.

LD students sometimes experience difficulty in social situations. For example, an individual with an auditory processing problem may misunderstand what others say or not understand the subtleties of conversation. Such misperceptions may cause the individual to respond inappropriately. A student with a disability that involves visual perception may misinterpret nonverbal cues or stand too close to other people, making them uncomfortable. In either case, the kinds of perceptual problems that affect students academically can also appear in social situations, thus making it difficult for some LD students to develop and maintain satisfying relationships.

The psychosocial problems that some students experience can cause them to develop a poor self-concept, dependence on others, stress, anxiety, and global negative feelings (Price, 1988). One intervention that has been successful with students who have such difficulties is participation in a support group. These groups, facilitated in most cases by professionals, offer students concrete strategies for identifying and altering their behaviors. They also give them opportunities to discuss their concerns and frustrations with peers.

Assessment

Identifying the academic needs of LD college students has been the object of very little research over the past twenty years. To compound the problem, there are few diagnostic tests with norms for the adult population, and those that do exist have been used inconsistently (Carlton and Walkenshaw, 1991).

Determining appropriate academic support is further complicated by the fact that LD college students come from a variety of educational backgrounds. Some were diagnosed early in their schooling. Others were not diagnosed until they enrolled in college. Resource rooms have been the most common way of serving LD students since the early 1970s, when P.L. 94–142 was implemented. It called for students to be served in the least-restrictive environment possible. There is tremendous variation in the amount and type of accommodation and academic support that students receive before they enroll in a college or university. While most students are totally mainstreamed and receive tutoring in a resource room several times a week, a very small percentage has all its major classes with a resource teacher. The type of academic background that a student has, in conjunction with intrinsic factors, such as motivation, largely determines the kind of support that the student will need in a postsecondary setting.

The service provider typically identifies a student's needs during an initial interview just before or soon after the student enrolls in college. At that time, the student should give the college a copy of his or her most recent individualized educational plan (IEP) from high school, a transcript, and a copy of the most recent diagnostic evaluation. Since by law students are reevaluated every three years, current information should be available.

During this interview, the service provider also assesses the student's study habits, skill levels, motivation, and academic and career plans. Inventories that can help to assess these characteristics are widely used. Some programs have access to placement information, such as a writing sample for the English program, and other schools administer placement tests in reading, composition, and mathematics to assess the skills of all entering students.

Diagnostic Testing. Few postsecondary institutions provide diagnostic testing, but they often refer students to community resources for testing. When testing is offered on campus, it is generally available only to students with no previous diagnosis who have been referred for a possible learning disability. Limited resources and staff generally prevent schools from retesting students with current documentation. Diagnostic testing in high school or college usually consists of tests measuring aptitude and achievement, such as the Woodcock-Johnson Psycho-Educational Battery—Revised (Woodcock and Johnson, 1989) and the Wechsler Adult Intelligence Scale—Revised (Wechsler, 1981). At the college level, Carlton and Walkenshaw (1991) found that few other tests were administered with any consistency nationally. Standardized and informal reading tests and writing assessments, spelling tests, and tests measuring visual and auditory perceptual abilities are incorporated into more comprehensive evaluations.

Scores and interpretations should be reviewed carefully to help the student and the service provider gain insight into how the student can capitalize on his or her strengths. For example, a student who has difficulty reading may at the same time have excellent listening skills that would enable the student to benefit from books on tape. Inadequate writing performance should be analyzed to determine what is causing the problem. Does the student have trouble with mechanics, organization, or the act of composing itself? The test results may give clues to the type of accommodations that will benefit the student. In the case of mechanical problems, instruction on how to use the computer and appropriate word processing and grammar-checking software may be helpful.

Often, the most useful way of assessing a student's academic needs is by working closely with the student or by talking with faculty members or service providers who work with the student. While diagnostic test results and high school experiences may lay the groundwork for determining appropriate accommodations, the postsecondary setting presents a whole new array of experiences to all students, and LD students may have more difficulty adjusting to the new demands than their nondisabled peers.

Some of the adjustments that college students are typically expected to make without much difficulty present serious roadblocks for the LD student. For example, a computerized library system can intimidate many students, but it can keep the student with a learning disability out of the library. The large volume of reading required in many classes can present serious problems to the student with a reading disability. Laboratory sections require students to work quickly and process information visually while making associations.

It is difficult to predict with accuracy all the areas in which a student may excel or have difficulty. The only way to get a truly accurate picture is to communicate with the student regularly concerning his or her progress in a particular course. If too much time elapses before the student receives assistance with problems in a particular class, he or she can become discouraged and depressed. LD students often do not seek help because they do not know what kind of accommodations they need.

Nontraditional Students. Nontraditional or older students present a unique set of considerations for the student services provider. Negative school experiences or insufficient financial resources prevented some of these students from considering attendance at a postsecondary institution. Others are returning to school after earlier attempts at advancing their education. Some are trying college for the second or third time and have great anxiety about reentering a school situation. These students often have a poor educational background, and since they have been out of school for a number of years, they may be lacking basic skills in mathematics and English.

Since the concept of learning disabilities was not introduced until the 1960s, LD individuals who attended school before then or during that period were generally not identified as having learning disabilities. These students had difficulty throughout their schooling, and they were usually considered to be either of low intelligence or unmotivated. This history of misdiagnosis may have left many of those who eventually enter college with low self-esteem and high levels of frustration.

A comprehensive intake questionnaire enables the student services professional to determine whether a returning adult could benefit from a complete diagnostic test battery. If the professional suspects a learning disability, the student should be referred for assessment.

Patton and Polloway (1992) point out that a wide range of opportunities is available to LD adults. Access to vocational experiences and training opportunities has grown in recent years. Many community colleges have instituted a wide array of LD support services. Helping a returning adult to find an appropriate educational setting and addressing psychosocial and personal needs are critical for his or her success.

Learning Disabilities Programs

A few schools have comprehensive service programs. These programs, for which the student is typically charged an extra fee, offer extensive tutoring, skill development classes, counseling, and advocacy.

Support programs are more common. This type of program, which is often decentralized, usually offers accommodations and counseling through the disability services office, while the other services, such as writing and reading laboratories, tutoring, and counseling services, are offered by other departments on campus. While many colleges have such decentralized services, it is important to recognize that the growing number of LD students on college campuses will increase the demand on these services (McGuire, Hall, and Litt, 1991). The authors just cited also point out that students' academic outcomes can differ with the type of services that they receive. Although the question has not been investigated empirically, the anecdotal evidence suggests that students may be more successful if the services that they receive address their individual needs and specific learning disabilities.

Small, private colleges often do not advertise that they have learning disability services. Nevertheless, some of these schools are able to serve LD students on a case-by-case basis. In some instances, students are served through developmental education departments or writing skills laboratories. These institutions often do not have a staff member with training in the area of learning disabilities, but small classes and individualized attention may enable self-motivated students to do well.

Admissions

The student services professional plays a major role in access for LD students at the postsecondary level starting with the admissions process. It is important for an appropriate professional, such as a learning disabilities specialist, to be involved in the admissions process. This individual can help admissions staff interpret records that may not indicate a student's true academic potential.

The admission of LD students to postsecondary institutions raises issues that warrant serious consideration by college personnel. While LD students have average to above-average intelligence, their high school transcripts may not always reflect their academic abilities. Scores on such tests as the Scholastic Achievement Test (SAT) or the Admissions College Test (ACT) may reflect an LD student's difficulties with computer-scored tests, multiple-choice questions, and other problems, not the student's ability. Although LD students are eligible to take these standardized tests with extended time, the nature of the test itself poses unique problems for them.

Scott (1990) explains that the student with a learning disability sometimes presents a challenge both for families and for college personnel by being "otherwise qualified," an expression meaning that there is often no standard way of reviewing the application of a student who has a learning disability. Many factors, such as college requirements, individual abilities, and reasonable accommodations, must be weighed and considered.

The number of LD students currently enrolled in colleges and universities is far lower than we should expect (Spillane, 1992). Although the discrepancy has not been investigated fully, the evidence suggests that schools are not taking advantage of important resources that could increase accessibility. The 1978 guidelines developed by the American Association of Collegiate Registrars and Admissions Officers (AACRAO) to assist postsecondary institutions in their efforts to respond to the letter and spirit of Section 504 offer information that is both valuable and very much needed. The AACRAO recommends that institutions establish advisory committees including individuals with expertise in disability and that they use the guidelines to review existing practices and develop policies and procedures that will increase access and participation by people with disabilities (Spillane, 1992).

Program Access

Section 504 of the Rehabilitation Act of 1973 and the Americans with Disabilities Act require postsecondary programs to provide program access to LD students. Institutions accomplish this aim by using support services, academic adjustments, and reasonable accommodations that help the student to compensate for his or her learning disability. It is important to recognize that accommodations are provided only to ensure equal opportunity. The LD student is not being given an advantage over other students. Auxiliary aids and services give LD students an opportunity to demonstrate their abilities in areas where their learning disability is an issue.

Accommodations. The student services provider who is responsible for providing learning disability programming must observe the requirements of Section 504 . As the number of LD students at the postsecondary level increases, the number of services also increases. Services typically include books on tape, time extension on tests, tutoring, and counseling. Some programs offer notetakers; readers and scribes for exams; distraction-free exam space; instruction in word processing; assistive computer technology, such as the Kurzweil Reading Machine; and peer support groups.

Brinckerhoff (1991) points out that some academic adjustments are programmatic in nature. His examples are priority scheduling, priority housing arrangements, and enrollment in remedial or developmental classes.

Academic Skill Building. Students in postsecondary settings are expected to have attained a certain level of academic skill. LD students generally have deficits in some combination of written language, reading, and mathematical skills. These deficits can be the result of learning disability. In some cases, they result from the absence of opportunities to participate in challenging classes at the middle and secondary school levels. Some LD students also lack study skills. Explicit instruction in this area is critical if students are to meet the demands of college (McGuire, Hall, and Litt, 1991).

Some postsecondary settings provide remedial courses in English and mathematics for all students. Writing centers and tutoring are also common. The service provider should be knowledgeable about the resources available on campus and network with staff in these programs so the needs of LD students can be addressed appropriately.

Support. In addition to helping students identify appropriate resources, the service provider must be able to help an LD student meet the challenges of academic life through counseling and support. LD students often have to work harder and longer hours than their peers. It is important for the service provider to help a student assess why something is not going well and to reject the conclusion that something is impossible. For every LD student, there are times when things do not go well. It is up to student services staff to provide an environment in which students feel comfortable admitting that they need help. In some cases, it becomes clear that a student cannot be successful in a particular setting. It is often the service provider who is responsible for helping the student to identify alternatives.

Curriculum Modifications. One academic adjustment that college administrators, faculty, and service providers have discussed in depth is curriculum modification, specifically in the form of course substitution. The two academic areas in which curriculum modification has most often become an issue are mathematics and second language. If the problematic class is not integral to the course of study, substituting a related course may be a reasonable academic adjustment (Brinckerhoff, 1991). For example, culture classes might replace the second language requirement, or logic and computer courses might be appropriate substitutions for the mathematics requirement. However, if the problematic course is a key part of the student's academic program, substitution is not an appropriate accommodation. Postsecondary educators and administrators should consider alternative ways of meeting a specific requirement in order to assure that a learning-disabled student earns a degree equal to that of his or her peers.

Collaboration with Faculty

One of the most important aspects of the student services professional's job is to serve as liaison between students and faculty. Success in a postsecondary setting depends not only on the student's academic skills but also on his or her ability to work effectively with faculty. Many LD students may need support and guidance to negotiate the academic setting.

It is important for faculty to know that a disability services office exists, what its functions are, and what kind of support they can expect from the office. One way of achieving this aim is by placing a description of the office and its functions in student handbooks, college catalogs, the student newspaper, directories of campus services, and other appropriate sources. A brochure describing services is also important.

Beyond the dissemination of written material, in-service for faculty and opportunities to meet with faculty formally and informally are also necessary. One successful way of meeting with faculty members is to request time at faculty meetings to describe services and answer questions. Another way to reach faculty is by offering workshops at times when faculty members are available. In-service can include simulation activities and discussion.

It is important to have written policies and procedures regarding testing accommodation. The disability services office should develop a form that states the amount of time allowed for an exam, the time and location of the exam, and any equipment (for example, calculator, computer) or materials that will be allowed. Having a written agreement ensures communication between faculty member and student—an important dimension of the student's success.

Recommendations for the Future

The last decade has brought an increasing number of LD students onto college campuses. Postsecondary institutions have expended much energy developing programs, training faculty, and offering students an array of services. Section 504 of the Rehabilitation Act in 1973 and the Americans with Disabilities Act in 1990 motivated the service expansion that we saw in the 1980s and early 1990s.

Every postsecondary institution should strive to maintain academic standards while accommodating LD students. This issue requires ongoing communication, and it must involve student services professionals as well as faculty and administrators. The student services professional must understand the manifestations of learning disability and the laws mandating that students shall not be discriminated against because of their disabilities.

Among the many areas that administrators and student service professionals must develop and operationalize are admission standards, academic adjustments, and curriculum modifications. McGuire, Norlander, and Shaw (1990, p. 71) point out that college personnel will be "challenged to review and revise policies which offer limited flexibility in meeting academic requirements." These challenges may include requests for waivers or substitutions in the areas of foreign language and mathematics. The authors just cited warn that institutions will need to know where to draw the line so that programs are not compromised.

There will be many challenges to postsecondary learning disability services in the next decade. As Hughes and Smith (1990) point out, postsecondary LD professionals have provided services and recommended accommodations with no empirical evidence of what does or does not work. With all that has been written about the heterogeneity of the LD population, there should be more consideration of the techniques and accommodations that might benefit particular students.

Instructional alternatives and existing techniques must also be studied carefully. Some students seem truly surprised when they do well in a course. They do not know whether their success was due to the type of material, the way in which it was presented, the teacher, their own study techniques, or something else. Classroom research requires a major commitment of time and resources, but it is pivotal to the success of LD students in postsecondary settings. Professionals in the field cannot continue to rely on self-reports if they want to help students reach their potential. It is time to start researching how LD students learn as individuals and why they sometimes cannot learn.

Program evaluation is another area that needs attention. Programs should evaluate the services that they offer in a systematic way. It is difficult to improve programming without consistent feedback from all the sources involved.

Finally, it is time to collaborate nationally to develop criteria for diagnostic procedures and identification of learning disabilities at the postsecondary level, to establish policies for curriculum modifications, and to improve services. As each school develops its own policies, procedures, and methods, it becomes increasingly difficult for students to traverse the system. Moreover, the variations that we can observe in the ways in which important decisions are made and carried out leave the impression that the field is not cohesive. What Scheiber and Talpers (1987) have found is true: LD students can be successful in a variety of settings. It is important now for professionals in postsecondary learning disability services to work together so that students may know what they can rightfully expect in any setting.

References

Brinckerhoff, L. "Establishing Learning Disability Support Services with Minimal Resources." *Journal of Postsecondary Education and Disability*, 1991, 9(1–2), 184–196.

Carlton, P. M., and Walkenshaw, D. "Diagnosis of Learning Disabilities in Postsecondary Institutions." *Journal of Postsecondary Education and Disability*, 1991, 9(1–2), 197–206.

Ganschow, L. "Analysis of Written Language of a Language Learning-Disabled (Dyslexic) College Student and Instructional Implications." *Annals of Dyslexia*, 1984, 34, 271–284.

Gregg, N. "College Learning-Disabled Writer: Error Patterns and Instructional Implications." *Journal of Learning Disabilities*, 1983, 16, 334–337.

Hartman, R. Foreword to Cathy Henderson (ed.), *College Freshmen with Disabilities: A Statistical Profile*. Washington, D.C.: American Council on Education, 1992.

Henderson, C. (ed.). *College Freshmen with Disabilities: A Statistical Profile*. Washington, D.C.:

American Council on Education, 1992.

Hughes, C. A., and Smith, J. O. "Cognitive and Academic Performance of College Students with Learning Disabilities: A Synthesis of the Literature." *Learning Disability Quarterly*, 1990, *13*, 66–79.

Kirk, S. *Educating Exceptional Children*. Boston: Houghton Mifflin, 1962.

Mangrum, C. T., II, and Strichart, S. S. *College and the Learning-Disabled Student*. Philadelphia: Grune & Stratton, 1988.

McGuire, J. M., Hall, D., and Litt, V. A. "A Field-Based Study of the Direct Service Needs of College Students with Learning Disabilities." *Journal of College Student Development*, 1991, *32*, 101–108.

McGuire, J. M., Norlander, K. A., and Shaw, S. F. "Postsecondary Education for Students with Learning Disabilities: Forecasting Challenges for the Future." *Learning Disabilities Focus*, 1990, *5*(1), 69–74.

National Joint Committee on Learning Disabilities (NJCLD). Letter to NJCLD member organizations. National Joint Committee on Learning Disabilities, 1988.

Patton, J. R., and Polloway, E. A. "Learning Disabilities: The Challenges of Adulthood." *Journal of Learning Disabilities*, 1992, *25*(7), 410–415.

Price, L. "Effective Counseling Techniques for LD Adolescents and Adults in Secondary and Postsecondary Settings." *Journal of Postsecondary Education and Disability*, 1988, *6*(3), 7–16.

Scheiber, B., and Talpers, J. *Unlocking Potential: College and Other Choices for Learning-Disabled People—A Step-by-Step Guide*. Bethesda, Md.: Adler and Adler, 1987.

Scott, S. S. "Coming to Terms with the 'Otherwise Qualified' Student with a Learning Disability." *Journal of Learning Disabilities*, 1990, *23*, 398–405.

Spillane, S. A. "Learning Disabilities and Admission Decisions: Resources and Requirements." *Latest Developments*, Fall 1992, pp. 3–4.

Vogel, S. A., and Moran, M. R. "Written Language Disorders in Learning-Disabled Students: A Preliminary Report." In W. M. Cruickshank and J. W. Learner (eds.), *Coming of Age: The Best of ACLD*, Vol. 3. Syracuse, N.Y.: Syracuse University Press, 1982.

Wechsler, D. *Wechsler Adult Intelligence Scale—Revised*. New York: Psychological Corporation, 1981.

Woodcock, R. W., and Johnson, M. B. *Woodcock-Johnson Psycho-Educational Battery—Revised*. Austin, Tex.: DLM Teaching Resources, 1989.

LYDIA S. BLOCK is coordinator of counseling and learning disability services in the Office for Disability Services at The Ohio State University, Columbus.

Disabled students of color face the stigma of double labels: disabled and minority. Service providers must improve their understanding of multicultural experiences if service to these populations is to improve.

Disabled Students of Color

Brenda Ball-Brown, Zelma Lloyd Frank

Students of color are significantly underrepresented in most college and university disability service programs. There are a number of reasons why students of color may not access disability services. Some involve cultural differences in perceptions of disability. Others result from historical precedent and language differences. Moreover, identification as both minority and disabled creates a double stigma. When a single individual embodies both concepts, the hurdles can often seem insurmountable.

The barriers that limit the effectiveness of services for this population mirror the society at large. Jenkins (1982, p. 87) made this point very clear when she stated: "minority students who are disabled may not think that they are treated or will be treated in an accepting and genuine manner . . . [U.S.] culture has a history of treating persons who are disabled in a very uncaring and insensitive manner as evidenced in the earlier practices of social Darwinism and eugenics. It is within this framework that the professional and disabled client, the powerful and the powerless, meet. They are very likely to be separated by race, money, education, language, social position, and lack of real knowledge of and feeling for the other's life experiences. They come together as mutual strangers with feelings of fear, suspiciousness, anger, and pain, which may cause each, the professional and disabled client, to become defensive. At the same time, they share a common need for each other. It is this commonality which makes it possible to overcome barriers to effective service delivery."

The literature indicates that few disabled students of color are accessing services. We need to ask why. This chapter addresses some of the issues that have a bearing on the answer. We begin by examining an additional difficulty that some disabled people of color bring to postsecondary education from their K–12 experience: unnecessary placement in special education programs. Because we are African Americans, we will focus on the experiences of that group. However, many of the issues for African American students are relevant for students from other minorities. Next, we address some general cultural differences that can affect both the response by people of color to disability services and the response from disability services to people of color. Last, we propose some guidelines for service provision.

It is important to note that ethnic groups, be they Hispanic, Native American, Asian, African American, or European American, are not monolithic. Within each, there are atheists and fundamentalists, conservatives and liberals, talkers and quiet people, and multitudes of other "types." We have chosen to highlight a narrow range of cultural differences. Service providers and postsecondary administrators should target their programs for more intense multicultural education, perhaps slightly emphasizing the populations that they are often likely to serve.

African American Students and Special Education

When African Americans (and often other minority students) experience academic difficulties early in their public education, they are often diagnosed as learning disabled, mentally retarded, or both. As Obiakor (1992, p. 160) observes, perception, race, gender, and class have a direct bearing on this determination: "Very often, African American students are judged as inferior based on the old theory of biological determinism . . . and are inappropriately classified, categorized, and placed in special education." And so the cycle begins.

Special education classes have had different names in different cities, states, and school districts. The stated reason for assessment and placement in such classes was to improve the educational outcomes for children. However, placement in a special education class often resulted not from the need to improve the educational outcome or accommodate a child's disability but to find alternative means and teaching methods for students needing instruction that could accommodate their cultural experiences and learning styles (Executive Committee of the Council for Children with Behavioral Disorders, 1989).

After enactment of P.L. 94–142, many school districts aggressively diagnosed, prescribed, and placed certain students, mainly minorities, in special self-contained education programs. MacMillan, Hendrick, and Watkins (1988) document these changes in identification and programming due to P.L. 94–142. The minority students who were placed in special classes were often misdiagnosed, and therefore they should never have been placed in the classes. The National Research Council Report (Heller, Holtzman, and Messick, 1982) revealed that a disproportionately high number of African American males were placed in special education classes. Moreover, the tests used to evaluate and diagnose are usually culturally biased. Hilliard (1992) points out that the overrepresentation of African American and Hispanic children in classes for students with educable mental retardation (EMR) raises serious issues regarding the diagnosis of mental retardation. These students might have made greater gains if they had been allowed to remain in regular classrooms. Some research has shown that students, when placed in any kind of special environment, tend to take on the behaviors of that group, positive or negative. Mainstreaming was based partially on that finding.

Once a student has been placed in a special education program, he or she often stays there, because little if any effort is made either to reassess students or to include them in mainstreamed programs. Our experiences and observations suggest that these classes are often further divided and categorized by specific levels of disability. Some labeling is necessary for tracking purposes, but the student, the student's peers, and family members usually perceive these labels as having negative connotations. Unfortunately, the labeling follows the students throughout their educational careers. Our experience is also that the level of expectation in these classes is often lower than it is in regular classes, and when less is expected, less is achieved. Add to this teachers' attitudes and an inadequate education, which can hinder students for a lifetime. A study by Aloia, Maxwell, and Aloia (1981, p. 622) indicated that "the race of the student significantly influenced the teachers' overall initial expectations and that the labeling significantly reduced teachers' initial impressions of intellectual potential. The labeling also tended to have a less negative effect on impressions of behavior of white students compared to African American or Mexican American students."

The labeling of minority students ensures the initiation of yet another negative identification. The student already faces discrimination because of skin color. The additional classification puts yet another basis for discrimination into place.

Picture a student of color who carries all the special education baggage and more who finally graduates from high school. With graduation comes a sense of accomplishment, hope, and new direction. If this student chooses postsecondary education, why not drop the previous debilitating, limiting, categorizing baggage of bygone days and move forward? Why carry it into a new era, a new evaluation, a new personal identification?

For the reasons just reviewed, there are students of color who enter postsecondary education with absolutely no desire to reveal any disabilities. The weight of their disability is already overpowering. Despite the mandate for self-advocacy in Section 504, few students of color decide to acknowledge their disability openly and get help before it is too late.

Cultural Differences

Cultural differences in the acceptance of disabilities are another key issue that affect how some students of color utilize disability services. The consequences of the intolerance and rejection that have beset minority cultures can translate into specific reasons for avoiding services. According to Jenkins (1982, p. 87), for example, "previous work with African American disabled students indicates that they are predisposed to dispositional barriers of fear, alienation, feelings about self and value orientation." Jenkins (1982, p. 88) further states that students are likely to have fears of "(1) self-disclosure: Can I trust the counseling staff? Will I be viewed as too passive or too aggressive? Will seeking services emphasize my disability more than my abilities? (2) loss of power over self: Will I lose control over my college experience? Will they manipulate or exploit me to make the office or college look good? Will they give any consideration to my wants? (3) being lied to: Will they only raise my hopes? Promise me assistance which will not be forthcoming? Will they lie by omission, i.e., not inform me of all the services for which I am eligible? (4) experiencing alienation: I will feel alienated because the situation is strange. I never planned to attend college. I don't know how to act. I can't look them in the eyes. I know they think I am lazy, dumb, and uncooperative. Do I really want to feel alienated? (5) failure: My life has been one failure after another. I will not attempt to succeed, because I am simply going to fail again."

These fears are a deterrent to the procedure for receiving disability services. Under Section 504, services can be received only after the student identifies the problem. Other, more specific differences can also affect service delivery. The remainder of this section examines differences in four areas: perceptions of disability, language barriers, family and community systems, and perceptions of service.

Perceptions of Disability. Cultural differences are often reflected in the way in which disability is perceived. Perceptions can in turn affect responses to disability services. For example, in the African American community there is a tendency to hide or cover up disability. Some Asian cultures view disability as the result of something done by one's ancestors and therefore as a symptom of spiritual weakness. Religious beliefs also have an impact on some portions of the Hispanic and Latino populations: "[Some] may believe that a person is disabled because it is 'God's will' or that an 'echizo' (spell) has been cast. In this instance, the reaction is resignation to the fate and/or to do penance" (Head, 1982, p. 106).

The perceptions that people have about the origins or meaning of disabilities affect their responses to it. In some cases, acknowledging a disability and seeking assistance may be very difficult and even devastating. In such cases, service providers may have to be willing to "work with the family and/or through the religion, that is, receiving support of the community, church, priest, or the healer/spiritualist, all commonly well respected" to provide adequate assistance to a student of a particular ethnic group (Head, 1982, p. 106). In general, if service providers conduct seminars and distribute educational materials in neighborhoods and community organizations, perceptions of disabilities will change.

Language Barriers. Language differences can erect a barrier between the service provider and the disabled student of color whose native language is not English. Hispanic and Asian Americans often encounter difficulty in this area.

From the perspective of customer service, first impressions based on language are common. People who are less than fluent speakers of English are sometimes assumed to be less intelligent than fluent speakers. They are spoken down to or spoken to loudly, in the patronizing way reserved for people with disabilities. However, a student's fluency in a second language depends on a variety of factors, which include age, access to structured English-as-a-second-language programs, and whether the student views learning English as a task that will actually create real opportunity for him or her in this country (Nichols, 1983). If the student can succeed within his or her community without a command of English, then spending time to acquire fluency could rationally be perceived as wasted. If lack of fluency is equated with lack of intelligence, the disabled student of color who is a nonnative English speaker will feel ostracized or patronized, and service delivery to such a student is not likely to succeed.

From the perspective of assessment, a student's proficiency in English can raise practical and complex questions. Is a student's difficulty in acquiring English due to the variables of age, lack of structured training, or lack of perceived advantage mentioned earlier, or does the student have a true learning disability? Given the prevalence of stereotyping and ethnically biased misdiagnoses of learning disabilities, if service providers rely on "impressions," it is likely that this complex question will not be answered satisfactorily. Once again, the disabled student of color is disadvantaged.

Communication styles can also cause miscommunication between students and service providers. For example, some Native Americans limit eye contact during a conversation out of respect for their interlocutor, and their physical contact with the person with whom they are conversing is also limited, again out of respect. Nonverbal skills are an important facet of communication within certain groups of Native Americans, and the members of these groups sometimes seem to be taciturn. Responses to questions may be very brief and use very few words. Some Asian American students avoid direct eye contact with authorities, which makes their interlocutors reluctant to ask or answer questions. African American students sometimes use an "insider" language that excludes those not part of the community (Jenkins, 1982).

Language is often a tool through which people retain and assert their ethnic identity. Service providers need to be aware that there are different varieties of English (such as Black English Vernacular and Spanglish), to issues involving the acquisition of English as a second language, and to differences in communication styles based in ethnicity. Failure to attend to linguistic differences can turn a student away from disability services. Language differences can be and have been misdiagnosed as learning disabilities, which can cast a student into a painful world.

Family and Community. Family and community are essential aspects of a student's life in many ethnic groups. Indeed, they may be so highly valued that they override the emphasis on individual success. For example, family ties are often strong in the Hispanic community. The whole family might get involved in the education process, and service providers must earn the trust of a wide range of individuals. "The family is the source of strength, the survival mechanism, the adviser, the counselor, and the center of social life. . . . when a Hispanic student makes an important decision, it is not his or her decision alone to make, but the unit, the family" (Head, 1982, p. 106).

In Native American communities, it is common to find three distinct types of family groups: first, a contemporary family reflecting the values and life-style typical of middle-class, majority culture; second, a semitraditional family in which parents practice cultural traditions, but the children, who have a strong sense of Indian identity, are not as knowledgeable about their culture and traditions as they would like to be; third, a traditional family, which often speaks the native language and observes cultural and religious traditions and values that reflect the family's tribal identity (S. Chapman, American Indian Student Support, Minnesota Community Colleges, Minneapolis, personal communication, 1993). "In tribal culture, the extended family or tribal community provides care and support for the person who is in need. That person, in turn, is expected to provide support to the tribal community and to the other family members when they are able . . . the concept of ownership by the entire community needs to be recognized" (Hermanson and Landstrom, 1991, p. 15). "The family is rather a multigenerational complex of people and clan and kinship responsibilities extended beyond the grave and far into the future" (Deloria, 1990, p. 160). As a result, disability is a concern of the whole community.

The role of family and community as a source of strength plays a vital part in the lives of many young adults. Barriers created by unwilling service providers can seem insurmountable. Transforming the student's perceptions of self and the world into feelings of confidence is a hard task, and the frustrations are great (Deloria, 1990). Service providers working with disabled students of color must be prepared to include the student's family. If they do not, it is likely that some students will not seek services.

Perceptions of Service. Perceptions of service programs often derive from past personal experience. For example, African Americans look on disability services as a continuation of the special education programs that they have experienced. They may ask whether they want to embrace a system that seems to be only an extension of one that has historically worked in opposition to them. Little if any gain will be made in the African American community if such a perception continues. To counter distrust, disability service providers have an obligation to educate the African American community about the differences between K–12 special education programs and the disability services provided by postsecondary education.

In the Asian American community, some students have an aversion to paperwork. Some feel that it intrudes on their privacy. For Vietnamese-Americans, it is a reminder of the fear that they experienced under Communist rule, a fear that also makes it difficult for those students to seek assistance from non-Asian service providers (Garner, 1991).

Some Native American students lack self-confidence and face a history of failure (Hermanson and Landstrom, 1991). They might not be aware of career options or of the other services that they might need if they are to reach their educational goals. Jarrow (1990) has observed that, when Native Americans enter postsecondary education, they often have had very little contact with professionals other than teachers, doctors, and in some cases clergy. As a result, they often are fearful, and they do not know where to go for assistance.

The diagnostic and referral system can create yet another barrier. The process can be long and impersonal. Students are sometimes sent to agencies off campus for evaluation, and this may require them to make appointments, use public transportation, stand in long lines, and be serviced by people who are less than cordial. The whole process can be threatening and intimidating, and students may choose not to utilize the diagnostic and referral system, especially minority students with disabilities who already distrust the system.

The perceptions of disability services by disabled people of color have rational bases in history. Service providers must be attentive to the differences that personal experiences can create. They must be sensitive to the roles that language, family, and perceptions of disabilities and services play in ethnic communities. In the next section, we propose some general guidelines that can help to develop such sensitivity.

Implications for Service Providers

The premise that all groups share some commonalities that can be used as a springboard for approaches to service delivery suggests that service providers and administrators can implement certain basic practices when working with disabled students of color. Principles suggested by Tidwell (1980) serve as a sound general model:

First, estimates of ability, personality, and behavior must come from assessment instruments that minimize socioeconomic, class, and cultural bias. Data from these instruments should not be the only criteria on which important educational decisions are based.

Second, the processes by which students learn social behavior should emphasize and value diverse cultural definitions of these behaviors.

Third, service providers should not devalue the cultural or racial heritage of students, staff members, or community.

Fourth, methods that are appropriate for students from one culture may not be appropriate for students from another culture, so service providers must help school staff to increase their sensitivities to the appropriateness of varying methods.

Fifth, the methods used should place a high priority on building a sense of personal worth in students, so they feel valued both as individuals and as members of particular cultural and racial groups.

Because student services administrators quite often set the tone for an entire institution, they must be knowledgeable about race, ethnicity, and disability. They must be actively involved in implementation and, whenever possible, design of the service delivery program. They must work to ensure that it has adequate funding and proper staffing. When they are working with disabled students of color, it is also important to involve administrators within the concerned cultural communities.

What can service delivery programs do to begin the process of multicultural inclusion? Here are some specific, basic answers:

First, whenever possible, hire culturally diverse staff to address and serve the needs of a diverse population of students with disabilities. Diverse staff can also be effective in disseminating program information to their communities and serving as community role models.

Second, include and encourage disabled students of color to exchange ideas and suggest ways of improving services.

Third, include carefully structured plans for career sampling and career development.

Fourth, provide outreach services to the members of the larger community. Conduct seminars and distribute educational materials about disabilities to neighborhood and community organizations. Churches, community agencies, and parent advisory groups all may be effective mechanisms for identifying talented youth who can be included in program activities. Working closely with the community is of utmost importance. Thus, programs need to be designed in ways that facilitate cooperative community involvement.

Fifth, be patient and sensitive to the individual needs of each student, and be appreciative of each individual's personal history and experience.

Sixth, develop workshops and training sessions for staff on communication styles and other language issues, such as stages of second language learning, bilingual education, and prejudicial beliefs about language.

Seventh, be prepared to work closely with students in developing short-range educational and money management plans with the understanding that they can become the basis for long-range plans.

Eighth, establish peer referral networks.

Ninth, encourage efforts to establish a national network of service providers for disabled students of color.

Tenth, financial aid issues are still a primary reason why students drop out. Thus, it is especially important for disability services to network with the financial aid office to facilitate access to adequate financial aid.

Eleventh, when assessing students of color, give careful consideration to the methods and instruments used to diagnose disabilities. Many of these tests err in one or both of two ways: They are culturally biased, and they assume that the population to be tested shares the same or similar experiences.

Twelfth, family involvement in all aspects of the student's educational career is an important element in the student's success. It is not enough that students understand their options. Those options must also be made acceptable to the family and community to whom the students answer (Western Educational Opportunity Personnel, 1990).

Summary

Many distinct but not always easily identifiable issues are related to the provision of disability services to students of color. The issues include but are not limited to cultural identity and stereotypes, historical precedent, language differences, learning styles, and self-concept or feelings of self-worth. All these factors contribute to the reluctance encountered among minority students to access services. The extent of this reluctance varies with circumstances and the specific population of minorities being served.

Service providers must be sensitive to the unique circumstances of students of color, for it is evident that the greatest deterrent to those who would access such services is prejudice against those in the society who are "different." Service providers and administrators must demonstrate effectiveness in educating a multicultural society. The authors agree with Hilliard (1992) that people of color experience the same needs for services as the majority population, that they are entitled to such services, and that appropriate services are services that are at once pedagogically valid and culturally sensitive and salient.

There has been much rhetoric about the commitment to serve disabled students of color. Until that rhetoric is translated into action, disabled students of color will continue to feel that they are in a class apart. The recent emphasis on multicultural diversity may change the focus so that disabled students of color will be sought aggressively and encouraged to use the services existing on college and university campuses.

References

Aloia, G. F., Maxwell, J. A., and Aloia, S. D. "Influence of a Child's Race and the EMR Label on Initial Impressions of Regular-Classroom Teachers." *American Journal of Mental Deficiency*, 1981, 85(6), 619–623.

Deloria, V. "Knowing and Understanding: Traditional Education in the Modern World." *Winds of Change: A Magazine of American Indians*, 1990, 5(1), 12–18.

Executive Committee of the Council for Children with Behavioral Disorders. "Best Assessment Practices for Students with Behavioral Disorders: Accommodation to Cultural Diversity and Individual Differences." *Behavioral Disorders*, 1989, 14(4), 263–278.

Garner, B. "Southeast Asian Culture and Classroom Culture." *College Teaching*, 1991, 37(4), 127–130.

Head, A. S. "Encountering Hispanic Disabled Students." *Handicapped Student Service Programs in Postsecondary Education: It Doesn't Cost, It Pays!* Proceedings of the 1982 AHSSPPE Conference. Columbus, Ohio: Association on Handicapped Student Service Programs in Postsecondary Education, 1982.

Heller, K. A., Holtzman, W. H., and Messick, S. (eds.). "Placing Children in Special Education: A Strategy for Equity." National Research Council Report. Washington, D.C.: Academy Press, 1982.

Hermanson, M., and Landstrom, B. "Developing a Sense of Community for Students with Disabilities at a Tribally Controlled College." *Osers News in Print*, Summer 1991, pp. 14–16.

Hilliard, A. G. "The Pitfalls and Promises of Special Education Practice." *Exceptional Children*, 1992, 59(2), 168–172.

Jarrow, J. *Multicultural Diversity and Learning Disabilities.* Columbus, Ohio: AHSSPPE, 1990.

Jenkins, A. E. "Encountering Black Students Who Are Disabled." *Handicapped Student Service Programs in Postsecondary Education: It Doesn't Cost, It Pays!* Proceedings of the 1982 AHSSPPE Conference. Columbus, Ohio: Association on Handicapped Student Service Programs in Postsecondary Education, 1982.

MacMillan, D. L., Hendrick, I. G., and Watkins, A. V. "Impact of Diann, Larry P, and PL 94–142 on Minority Students." *Exceptional Children*, 1988, 54(5), 426–432.

Nichols, P. "Linguistic Options and Choices for Black Women in the Rural South." In B. Thorne, C. Kramarae, and N. Henley (eds.), *Language, Gender, and Society*. N.p.: Newbury House, 1983.

Obiakor, F. E. "Self-Concept of African American Students: An Operational Model for Special Education." *Exceptional Children*, 1992, 59(2), 160–167.

Tidwell, R. "Counseling in a Multicultural School System." *Journal of Nonwhite Concerns in Personnel and Guidance*, January 1980, pp. 84–90.

Western Educational Opportunity Personnel (WESTOP). *Serving Multiculturally Diverse Populations in TRIO Programs: A Beginners Guide from WESTOP*. Columbus, Ohio: Association on Handicapped Student Service Programs in Postsecondary Education, 1990.

BRENDA BALL-BROWN *is director of Project Access: Talent Search at the University of New Orleans and past president of the Association on Higher Education and Disability* (AHEAD).

ZELMA LLOYD FRANK *is director of student support services at Southern University at New Orleans and editor of* AHEAD's *bimonthly newsletter* The Alert.

*Student affairs administrators and staff need an appreciation of the
role that assistive computer technology can play in efforts to create
barrier-free environments.*

Assistive Computer Technology: Opening New Doorways

Carl Brown

In today's colleges and universities, instructional technology, computers, and
education are joined in a powerful and complex relationship that is rapidly
transforming our fundamental beliefs about the nature and process of instruction. The tidal wave of technology that is sweeping higher education into the next
century will leave behind those who are unable to access or employ the productivity enhancement tools that are becoming a daily fact of life on most campuses. Students with disabilities whose functional limitations make computer
access difficult or impossible are in grave danger of being pushed aside.

The term most widely used to describe both the hardware and software
that provide computer access for students with disabilities is *assistive computer
technology*. Assistive computer technology is academia's response to a nationally perceived need to bring students with disabilities into the technological
mainstream of campus activity. The Americans with Disabilities Act (ADA),
the Technology-Related Assistance Act, Section 508 of the Rehabilitation
Act, and the revised language of the Rehabilitation Act of 1973 all provide a
clear and unmistakable message to student services administrators and faculty: Now is the time for people with disabilities to have equal access to computer technology.

To help readers understand the history, concept, and future of assistive
computer technology in postsecondary education, this chapter examines the
development of the network of eighty-one High Tech Centers for the Disabled
in California community colleges. The High Tech Centers program provides a
well-established, large-scale model that we can use to examine the diverse
philosophical, academic, technical, organizational, and managerial issues associated with the academic use of assistive computer technology.

New Directions for Student Services, no. 64, Winter 1993 © Jossey-Bass Publishers

This chapter also provides student services administrators and staff with a body of information about the basic computer access needs of students with disabilities and the hardware and software required to meet those needs. Intended to help readers become more knowledgeable consumers and users of a new and sometimes confusing array of technologies, this chapter explores such issues as training and support for students, faculty, and staff; funding; purchase and maintenance of equipment; technology integration; professional competence; legal considerations; and the future of assistive computer technology.

From Where Have We Come?

Early in 1983, the disabled student services program at Monterey Peninsula College, like programs at many other California community colleges, was struggling with the complex issues of computer use in postsecondary education. In addition to matters of academic viability, cost-effectiveness, technical support, and instructional content, there was a more immediate question: What role would computers play in the lives of students with disabilities?

In spring 1984, the college offered its first courses in word processing for students with disabilities. Six students enrolled. The difficulty of using microcomputers, even by students with relatively mild orthopedic disabilities, was obvious. For example, how could a student who had only one finger to type with hold down two keys at once, as was sometimes required? How could a student with low vision see what was on the computer screen?

Through trial and error, college staff identified some partially effective solutions for some of the more acute access difficulties. Feeling confident that the computer access problem had been resolved, the college resumed the word processing course. In the following semester, fourteen disabled students enrolled in the course. Pleased that students with disabilities had accepted the new program, the instructor solved a few more computer access needs and proceeded to teach word processing. In the summer, more than thirty disabled students requested enrollment. Persons with disabilities who had never considered postsecondary education were enrolling at Monterey Peninsula College in order to learn word processing with assistive computer technology, and they were staying on to become successful participants in mainstream courses.

Demand for the course quickly overtook the program's ability to provide services. Close examination revealed that students were coming not just for word processing but for an opportunity to learn how to use assistive devices that gave them better access to computers in general. After careful consideration, it was determined that Monterey Peninsula College needed a systematic program of identification, testing, implementation, and instruction in assistive computer technology. Rather than build a new program by acquiring existing "traditional" assistive devices, program staff elected to determine what an ideal assistive computer device ought to do and then set out to find or create it.

The time was right for a radical change from the conventional methods for providing computer access to people with disabilities. As the primary goal, staff sought to replace expensive hardware-based computer modifications (such as special keyboards or large-screen display monitors) with high-quality, software-based adaptations. Keeping the demonstrated computer access needs of students with disabilities in mind, staff formulated a set of criteria for evaluating possible assistive computer technologies.

Every adaptation that the High Tech Center employed would function, wherever possible, entirely as software. It would give individuals with disabilities significantly improved access to microcomputers. It would function with industry standard software, such as Lotus 1–2-3, WordPerfect, and dBASE. It would share computer memory harmoniously with many other adaptations (students often needed to use several adaptations simultaneously for effective computer access). It would be easy to teach, learn, and maintain (with rare exceptions, the individual should have a basic grasp of program operation in less than thirty minutes). It would be affordable; that is, it would cost less than three hundred dollars. And it would function with MS-DOS or Macintosh computers (although we did not necessarily require particular adaptations to be interchangeable between DOS and Macintosh computers).

The High Tech Center was conceived of as a training facility, not as a separate but equal computer facility for students with disabilities. Students were expected to come to the High Tech Center to learn how to use the assistive computer technologies that were appropriate to their disability. A student who had attained a functional level of competence was expected to make the transition into mainstream courses where, if computers were used, assistive computer technology would be available. Staff felt that the transition of students into a wide range of courses that used computers (accounting, drafting, graphics, word processing, computer science) would give disabled students many other career opportunities in addition to computer programming.

Over the next two years, word of the program's success spread—first to neighboring community colleges, then to colleges across the state. There was soon a steady stream of visitors to the program. Visiting faculty often occupied more than half the seats in the classroom. A series of events late in 1985 permanently altered the future of computer access for students with disabilities in the California community colleges.

After several visits to the High Tech Center, representatives from the Department of Disabled Students Programs and Services (DSP&S) in the office of the chancellor of the state community college system determined that the program was a valuable resource that should be made available statewide. The chancellor's office proposed establishing a large-scale research, evaluation, and training facility, the High Tech Center Training Unit, located in Sacramento, which would be available to DSP&S program directors and staff at all 107 California community colleges.

At roughly the same time, the California state Department of Rehabilitation (DR) became convinced that improved computer access could be of great benefit to its clients who were enrolled in community colleges. The cost-effectiveness and software transparency of the High Tech Center approach solved many of the access problems that the DR had encountered with computers in the past. The DR was also particularly interested in the capacity of assistive technology to provide important new avenues of opportunity for persons with acquired brain injuries or learning disabilities.

Early in 1986, the DR identified a federal establishment grant as a funding mechanism that could enable it to place assistive computer technology hardware and software and instructional staff at several California community colleges. Through a cooperative undertaking between the California state DR and the California community colleges chancellor's office, an innovative interagency plan was developed that met the needs of both agencies.

The model for creating establishment grant–funded High Tech Center programs was based on a standardized package of assistive computer hardware and software developed and tested at Monterey Peninsula College. Providing colleges with a fixed array of equipment made the complex task of training and providing technical support manageable. Faculty support and training were, and continue to be, mainstays of the High Tech Centers.

Successful introduction of assistive computer technology into a postsecondary setting requires much more than just the purchase of equipment. Several additional layers of support must be available in addition to formal training in the use of assistive and instructional technology. The High Tech Center Training Unit continues to provide a wide variety of training opportunities, telephone support, site visits, a statewide electronic bulletin board system, and advanced levels of technical support for hardware and software operation.

As of this writing, High Tech Center programs are in place at eighty-one California community colleges. All programs are funded locally, and they continue to grow and expand. On any given day, more than six thousand students with disabilities are enrolled in community college High Tech Centers.

Some twenty-five other states have begun programs based on the High Tech Centers model. Perhaps most significant, the computer access technology implemented by the High Tech Centers influenced development of Section 508 of the Rehabilitation Act, and it may serve as a guideline for determining appropriate workplace accommodation technologies mandated by the ADA.

What Are Assistive Computer Technologies?

As in other areas of computing and instructional technology, the variety of assistive computer products available for students with disabilities increases almost daily. Any attempt to identify and discuss specific products in the static environment of a sourcebook chapter is doomed to obsolescence. A better approach for managers, users, and consumers of these technologies is to have a good understanding of the special needs that these products are intended to meet and a general sense of how well they currently do the job. Such an understanding will provide greater long-term benefit to administrators, faculty, and consumers who employ these technologies.

Since each type of disability (for example, blindness, physical disability, learning disability) has its own unique computer access needs, the pages that follow explore access requirements by disability group and the current state of the art in assistive computer technology for each group.

Blindness. Sighted individuals use a variety of visual techniques when viewing text on a computer screen: A quick glance takes the reader to an interesting sentence or typing error. Reading speeds up for lengthy documents and slows down for critical analysis. Columns of figures are scanned to check a total. A quick look at the program menu confirms a system prompt or selection option. In order to make computers accessible to people who are blind, assistive technology must provide nonvisual alternatives for these tasks.

There are three ways of accomplishing this aim: Screen-reading software and sophisticated speech synthesizers can be used to make the screen display available in an auditory mode. A refreshable braille display can be used to echo the screen display in a tactile mode. Or, perhaps most dynamically, the two methods can be combined.

Since not all blind individuals read braille, this discussion centers on screen-reading software and speech synthesizers. Such systems allow the blind computer user to "see" the screen with his or her ears and to employ many of the same "visual" techniques used by sighted computer users.

The function of any screen-reading system is to become the "eyes" of the blind computer user. Screen readers provide their users with elegant and sophisticated ways of examining the content of the computer screen. What is "seen" on the screen is sent to the speech synthesizer. The speech synthesizer is a hardware device that translates ASCII code into spoken English. Like screen-reading systems, speech synthesizers are available from many sources and range in output quality from barely understandable robotic utterances to well-modulated voices that have all the inflections and nuances of human speech.

Beyond the relatively simple process of translating screen displays into spoken English, there are a number of considerations that a screen-reading program should take into account if it is to be a genuinely effective tool for a blind computer user. These considerations can be grouped under two headings: personal considerations and software considerations.

To judge the match between a screen-reading program and personal considerations, we need to ask such questions as these: Is the blind individual a competent touch typist? For obvious reasons, the two-finger hunt-and-peck method of typing is not a viable alternative for blind computer users. How well does the individual hear and understand the speech synthesizer? The question is important, because on the answer depends how well the user will understand what is displayed on the computer screen.

As for software considerations, screen-reading software should at all times provide a high degree of interactive reading capability. The majority of screen-reading systems operate in two modes: review and application. For example, on entering review mode in a word processor, the full range of the software's capabilities can be used to read the document displayed on the screen, but the document cannot be edited. In application mode, the word processor functions normally, but only a limited selection of screen-reading options is available. The best screen readers make most if not all screen-reading capabilities available in both review mode and application mode.

The software should be capable of reading letters, words, lines of text, complete sentences, paragraphs, screens, and complete documents. Just as sighted computer users scan written documents to obtain a sense of their overall continuity and flow, screen readers must give blind computer users options that allow these same processes to occur in an auditory mode.

A screen reader should also, at the user's discretion, provide spoken output for the prompts and messages displayed by the computer system or program in use. Computer programs, especially those that provide remote access to other computer systems through networks or via modem, often display messages and prompts regarding elapsed time, system charges, waiting messages, additional information to be displayed, and a number of other items. The user is interested in all these messages and prompts, and a screen reader must be able to monitor them and announce them when they appear.

A screen-reading system should provide a method for identifying the attributes of text displayed on the screen—bold, underlined, inverse, or color—as well as capital letters, punctuation marks, and diacritical marks.

A screen-reading system should provide user-defined screen locations that can be accessed instantaneously. Most computer programs include screen designs that incorporate menu selection areas, help screens, information display areas, and, in the case of spreadsheets, columns of numbers that must be read vertically. The solution to reading these specialized screen areas involves the creation of user-defined viewing areas called *windows*.

The software should provide on-line, spoken help screens and documentation in recorded, braille, and/or print formats as well as a user support hot line.

Low Vision. The text displayed on the normal computer screen is far too small to be read easily by individuals whose vision is limited. The obvious answer is to make the text larger.

Although the computer access needs of visually impaired computer users are readily apparent, there are a number of additional considerations that are less obvious but of equal importance. The ideal low-vision system should provide the following eight capabilities: First, it should produce a range of text magnifications from 1.5 to perhaps 10. Second, the large-print adaptation must be capable of full screen magnification of both text and graphics. Third, the large-print adaptation should work with monochrome, color, or enhanced color display environments, and it must preserve colors accurately in magnified form. Fourth, the large-print adaptation should be software based or entirely self-contained within the computer. Fifth, low-vision adaptations must be compatible with commercially available software. Sixth, the low-vision system should produce a fast, smooth display of enlarged text or graphics. When the viewing area is moved rapidly from one location to another, the system should display text quickly and smoothly, not in erratic jerks. Seventh, the large-print system should allow the user to modify the foreground and background colors. Eighth, the system should give the user options for tracking the cursor, highlight, or mouse pointer.

Orthopedic Disabilities. Orthopedic disabilities can impair mobility in a variety of ways. The assistive technology discussed in this section applies to people who are able to press all the keys on a standard computer keyboard with their fingers, their toes, or a pointing device held in their mouth or attached to their head. For people with physical disabilities, productive use of computers should address three critical issues: keyboard positioning, keyboard access, and typing speed.

Correct keyboard positioning allows persons with mild to moderate levels of orthopedic disability to minimize physical exertion and thus reduce fatigue. Properly positioned keyboards also decrease the spasticity and resultant keyboarding errors that can occur from straining to reach portions of the keyboard.

Assistive technologies that provide keyboard access are vitally important. The multiple keystroke commands common to many computer applications can pose an obstacle to persons with virtually any degree of orthopedic disability. For example, how can a one-handed typist or headstick user hold down a key on the left-hand side of the keyboard and simultaneously press a second key on the right-hand side of the keyboard?

Some of the most useful access tools available for individuals with orthopedic disabilities are programs that give them control over keyboard operation. For many persons with orthopedic disabilities, use of such an adaptation may be all that is required to gain access to computers. Keyboard control programs should meet five criteria: First, they should always be software based. This facilitates access and allows the user to move easily from one computer to another. Second, keyboard control programs should be capable of turning off or modifying the key repeat function. Third, keyboard control programs must be capable of electronically "latching down" the Ctrl, Alt, and Shift keys individually or in combination. As already mentioned, commands requiring users to press several keys at one time create a significant barrier for one-handed or touch-stick computer users. Keyboard control programs should also provide an automatic release feature to "unlatch" these special keys after a second, non-special key has been pressed. Fourth, for moderately orthopedically disabled computer users, one of the most frustrating aspects of using a physical keyboard is the unintentional pressing of keys as a result of tremor, spasticity, or limited fine motor control. Keyboard control programs that can modify the length of time for which a key must be held down before it is activated "desensitize" the keyboard and greatly reduce typing errors. Fifth, keyboard control programs should operate with standard commercial software and give users a way of having them start up automatically every time the computer is turned on.

Persons whose disabilities prevent them from typing at a rate greater than ten or twelve words per minute may benefit from assistive technologies that enhance the rate of text production. Word completion programs that make surprisingly accurate predictions about word choice while a sentence is being written are one solution. Such systems can predict the rest of the word being written generally after the first or second letter of the word has been typed. The user is shown a list of likely choices, and he or she can elect to complete the word or phrase by pressing a single key. Such systems also automatically manage the tasks of inserting the correct number of spaces after punctuation marks and beginning a new sentence with a capital letter. Word prediction programs should operate transparently with commercial software applications, allow the user to add new words and phrases on the fly, and constantly adjust word use frequency tables to enhance the speed and accuracy of word prediction.

Within the last two years, great strides have been made in the development of accurate, fast, large-vocabulary speech recognition systems for microcomputers. Speech recognition systems can serve as a supplement or even as a replacement for data entry on a physical keyboard. To function effectively, they require very high degrees of accuracy and reliability. High-end speech recognition systems are capable of producing text reliably at perhaps thirty-five to forty words per minute with around 95 percent accuracy.

Learning Disabilities. Approximately 5 to 10 percent of any given population experiences mild visual, auditory, or tactile-kinesthetic processing deficits of a neurological origin commonly known as *learning disabilities*. These deficits affect a student's ability to acquire, integrate, and express information. For a student in postsecondary education or an employee in a text-oriented occupation (for example, word processing), the effects of this disability can be significant.

For some, all that may be needed to improve productivity is a simple spelling checker and correction program used in conjunction with the computer application. Many individuals with learning disabilities may also benefit from real-time spelling checker programs. As soon as a real-time spelling checker program detects a spelling error, it prompts the writer and displays the correct spelling.

Persons whose visual processing deficits make identification of grammar or spelling errors difficult are often able to correct such errors by reviewing text auditorily. Screen-reading systems tailored to the special requirements of persons with learning disabilities can be effective in increasing their productivity. Screen-reading systems intended for blind computer users can also be adapted for use by persons with learning disabilities.

These adaptations can be used in combination with other assistive computer technologies to meet the needs of people with severe learning disabilities. By employing a combination of adaptations, including word prediction programs, real-time spelling checkers, screen-reading systems, and advanced speech synthesizers, we can create a writing environment that is multisensory rather than visually oriented. In this environment, word prediction software working in conjunction with a word processor can suggest appropriate words or phrases, correct spelling automatically, and have the user hear as well as see what he or she has written.

Although there are no simple solutions to the needs of persons with learning disabilities, computers can be used to create a working environment that can compensate for or reduce the effects of visual, auditory, tactile, and kinesthetic processing deficits.

Deafness and Aural Impairment. Many computer programs use various tones or beeps to alert the user to error conditions, work completion, or other events. Deaf or hard-of-hearing people must have access to these cues. The solution is visual cues for auditory prompts. The system should provide a highly visible prompt (such as a message, flashing screen, icon, or other symbol) to notify the hearing-impaired user of events marked by audible signals. The user should be able to define the duration, color, and location of such prompts.

What Have We Learned?

After eight years of program operation, what have we learned about the operation and management of High Tech Center programs? This section groups the discussion of our learnings under three heads: staff training, equipment purchase and maintenance, and technology integration.

Staff Training. California community college High Tech Centers are operated by a diverse array of full- and part-time staff ranging from tenured faculty specializing in speech and language, learning disabilities, special education, and related fields to instructional aides. The staff configuration of these programs is influenced by a variety of factors, including funding, institutional commitment, program delivery models, classroom space, equipment availability, and student demand.

Early High Tech Center programs were almost always staffed by at least a half-time faculty member. Over time, we have seen these programs remain academically sound and stably funded. They continue to address a wide array of computer access needs of students with disabilities. The level of professional expertise that faculty bring to High Tech Center programs lends academic credibility and supports the development of well-integrated, functional programs.

Under another model that has emerged in recent years, High Tech Center programs are operated entirely by instructional aides. In contrast to programs staffed by faculty, which are often structured around formal courses listed in the college catalog, this model is much more informal and takes the form of individualized, rather than classroom-based, instruction. Although instructional aides often lack degrees, they receive the same training in assistive computer technology as their faculty counterparts. Often, these aides are college staff who were already working in instructional technology or computer labs as support personnel. Much in the way in which a lab technician can help a student learn to use a word processor or campus e-mail system, these staff members help students to understand the mechanics of using a particular assistive device.

Each staffing configuration has advantages and disadvantages. Perhaps the best approach is to combine faculty with instructional aides. In this model, a full- or part-time faculty member uses his or her professional skills and experience to determine the students' computer access needs and then provides formal classroom instruction. Instructional aides operating in the college's instructional technology or computing laboratories provide ongoing support as students make the transition into mainstream facilities.

Independent of the model that is adopted, student services administrators must understand that, in contrast to more established academic disciplines, the field of assistive computer technology is a rapidly evolving specialty that requires somewhat more ongoing training than other fields do in order to retain currency. Unfortunately, there are as yet no formal licensing programs certifying professional competence in the field of assistive computer technology. Any thoughtfully conceived plan for the creation and maintenance of such a program must therefore include ongoing staff training to assure competence.

Equipment Purchase and Maintenance. Equipment is an essential component of any High Tech Center program. Selecting assistive hardware and software carefully matched to the needs of the student population is critical for success. The computers and assistive technologies that are purchased must be compatible with the hardware and software used in the college's mainstream computing facilities. Wherever possible, the college should standardize the large-print display system, keyboard control program, and other assistive technologies that will be used everywhere on campus. Standardization will greatly facilitate the transition of students with disabilities into mainstream courses and streamline the installation and support of assistive technology across the campus.

When considering what and how much assistive computer technology to purchase, begin by reviewing the demographics of the institution's students with disabilities. Developing an understanding both of the numbers of students with particular disabilities and of their course-taking patterns can give you valuable information about how to distribute your institution's fiscal resources.

Like all hardware and software, assistive computer technology must be upgraded or replaced periodically. Any High Tech Center budget should include funds for that purpose. For the most part, three to five years of productivity can be anticipated from these technologies before software improvements or mechanical failures warrant replacement. Inevitably, the question of funding must be addressed. Whose responsibility is it to purchase and maintain the equipment, hire and train staff, provide classroom space, and meet operating costs? The easy answer is to place this responsibility with the campus disabled student services program. However, the language of the ADA suggests that accountability for the provision of these services does not rest with a single program or even with a single department.

Providing access to classroom and workplace accommodation technologies for students, faculty, and staff with disabilities rests with the institution as a whole. In viewing equal access to educational and employment opportunity as a civil right that is likely to require the provision of assistive technology, institutions of higher education—student services administrators in particular—must rethink traditional methods of providing these accommodations. When the purchase of computer systems or instructional technology is being planned, planners must consider how such systems will be made accessible to students and staff with disabilities. To address this issue, some colleges have begun earmarking a small but fixed percentage of all instructional equipment moneys for such purchases.

Technology Integration. How assistive computer technology makes its way from the High Tech Center to campus computing or instructional technology centers is extremely important. In some respects, the college model that permits trained staff to deliver access training on an informal basis as needed may actually promote technology integration. These programs often operate in already existing computing or instructional technology facilities where access to mainstream computing is the norm.

More formal High Tech Center programs that have their own classrooms, curricula, hardware, and software systems must address the need to transition students, technical expertise, and assistive technology to campus computing facilities at large. It is perilously easy for students with disabilities, faculty, and student services administrators to allow High Tech Centers to become an institution's sole response to computer access for students with disabilities. Institutions that by design or oversight take this course of action may find themselves in difficulty with requirements both of Section 504 of the Rehabilitation Act of 1973 and of the Americans with Disabilities Act, which speak to least-restrictive environment and the avoidance of separate but equal facilities for persons with disabilities.

In addition to open computer and instructional technology labs, we must consider how we will provide assistive technologies in classrooms that employ computers as part of instructional methodology. Given the range and diversity of course offerings on the one hand and of the types of disability on the other, this challenge will require both compromise and sensitivity from all involved.

In large measure, the success of efforts to integrate assistive computer technologies campuswide rests on how well technical support staff, faculty, and administrators accept these technologies. Acceptance will require a good deal of discussion, training, and support aimed at helping staff to understand both the institution's legal obligations and the great benefit that assistive technologies represent to people with disabilities. Ideally, these discussions will result in comprehensive planning that addresses start-up and ongoing costs, space requirements, staffing, training, support, and service delivery methods.

Training is a requirement that will affect students with disabilities as well as a surprising number of other campus personnel. An individual or core group will need to receive initial as well as ongoing training in the use of assistive computer technologies. In addition to training students with disabilities, these individuals will need to pass their knowledge along to the members of several other campus groups, most notably technical support staff, faculty, counselors, and administrators. Each of these groups has a distinct role to play: technical support in the installation and day-to-day maintenance of the technology; faculty in student instruction and support for access technologies in computer-based classrooms; counselors in student identification, referral, and follow up; and administrators in staffing, funding, capital outlay, and facilities planning.

Where can training in the use of assistive computer technologies be found? Training centers are beginning to spring up nationwide. For the last several years, grants awarded under the Technology-Related Assistance Act have been funding the development of state resource centers intended to provide basic information and instruction in assistive computer technologies. Most states either now have or are currently developing such centers. Each year, two major conferences (Closing the Gap at the University of Minnesota and the California State University at Northridge conference in Los Angeles) attract thousands of users, vendors, faculty, and administrators from around the world who wish to learn more about assistive computer technology. Still, at the present time, it is far easier to acquire information about assistive technologies than it is to find a source for in-depth, hands-on professional training. The shortage of training centers may represent an opportunity for student services administrators in postsecondary education to establish cooperative projects with business and industry for the development of such facilities. In the years ahead, as both the public and the private sectors seek answers and expert information regarding the workplace accommodations and technologies required by the ADA, such centers could prove to be an invaluable resource.

A clearly stated, well-defined policy of programmatic, instructional, and fiscal support for campus assistive computer technology will establish a strong foundation for the development of such programs. There is no right or wrong way of addressing these needs. Each college or university must develop an approach appropriate to its unique academic and student requirements. Students with disabilities must understand that the institution is committed to their academic success and that it will provide all necessary and reasonable accommodations. Students with disabilities must also understand that the institution fully expects them to perform the essential functions of the job as students once these reasonable accommodations have been provided.

What Will the Future Be?

Campus computing, instructional, and assistive technologies continue to evolve. As the technology of interactive multimedia develops, the distinctions between computing, television, and graphic arts will blur into history. Computer interface design and how we interact with computing and instructional technology are undergoing a major transition. Speech recognition technology capable of operating computer applications and dictating text will be inexpensive and widely used within the next three to five years. The expansion and commercialization of existing global information networks will bring the world into the classroom and revolutionize thinking about time and distance.

How these new technologies and instructional resources affect the lives of students with disabilities remains to be seen. For many, dramatic advances in distance learning and telecommuting will bring added independence and competitive employment opportunities. For others, particularly students with visual disabilities, the highly graphic environments of the new multimedia computers will pose a challenge demanding a fresh generation of assistive computer technologies. Successful introduction of these new learning and productivity tools in ways that benefit the entire campus community will require understanding, thoughtfulness, and sensitivity from both faculty and administration.

In the coming years, as the courts interpret the legal implications of the ADA, colleges and universities may find themselves needing to consider a new range of fiscal, employment, and instructional responsibilities in providing access to technology and the workplace for students and staff with disabilities. In considering the institution's responsibilities for reasonable accommodation, there can be little doubt that they will include assistive technologies of one sort or another. How the institution will determine the essential requirements of the job, the functional limitations of the student or staff member, the accommodations to be made, and the funding sources for these services are questions requiring immediate planning and careful thought.

For example, it is easy to see how essential requirements of the job in a postsecondary setting might include the course content as well as the activities traditionally specified in a job description. Clearly, colleges and universities cannot use students' disabilities to restrict course enrollment. The steps that ought to be taken to inform students of the essential requirements of a course and the assistive technologies that can provide accommodation are urgent questions for faculty and administrators.

As postsecondary education moves to embrace technology as a strategy for reducing the cost of instruction, it will need to pay close attention to the hidden cost of assuring that these resources are also accessible to students with disabilities. Designs for the development of computing centers, learning centers, advanced technology centers, and libraries will undoubtedly include computers and instructional systems. A reasonable percentage of all equipment in these new facilities must be accessible to students and staff with disabilities. Planning for the inclusion of both architectural and assistive computer technologies from a project's inception is the wisest course of action.

Students with disabilities are rapidly becoming knowledgeable and sophisticated users of assistive computer technologies. In the California community college system alone, more than six thousand students with disabilities receive training in the High Tech Centers programs every year. Many of these students transfer to four-year colleges and universities as skilled users of assistive technology, able to advocate for their needs and fully expecting access to campus computing and instructional technology facilities. Such students represent an invaluable resource, for they bring with them the simple yet powerful assumption that they will be equal partners in the future of their colleges, companies, and country. Student services administrators and faculty have a unique opportunity to make certain that this assumption becomes a reality.

CARL BROWN is director of the California Community Colleges High Tech Center Training Unit in Cupertino, California, and author of Computer Access in Higher Education for Students with Disabilities.

This chapter assesses the accomplishments of the past two decades and outlines critical issues that must be addressed if both the spirit and the letter of the Americans with Disabilities Act are to be implemented on our college and university campuses.

Moving Ahead: Issues, Recommendations, and Conclusions

Sue Kroeger, Judy Schuck

We and the other contributors to this volume have analyzed the participation of students with disabilities in postsecondary education and assessed the progress that institutions of postsecondary education have made in including these students in the academic experience. We conclude, first, that institutions have not reached all disabled students and that they have reached some students inadequately; second, that funding at individual institutions for disabled student services is either nonexistent or inadequate; third, that nondisabled faculty, staff, and students receive insufficient training about disability, the ADA, and related issues; fourth, that the number of students on campus with hidden disabilities (that is, learning, psychiatric, systemic disabilities) is increasing rapidly and presents unique access issues and challenges for institutions; fifth, that disabled students of color are not represented in any significant way on campuses and that disability service offices are not serving those who do enroll; sixth, that earlier impact is needed to reverse the high dropout and low college-going rate for disabled secondary students; seventh, that students with disabilities whose limitations make computer access difficult are in danger of being left behind by the evolution of campus computing and instructional technology.

Increased awareness and demand as a result of the Americans with Disabilities Act (ADA) will require participation and cooperation by many units in order for colleges and universities to respond effectively to a diverse population of students and to demonstrate good faith efforts that they are working toward a barrier-free environment.

Issues and Recommendations

The issues and recommendations set forth in this section can help college and university administrators address the concerns expressed in the preceding section and implement both the spirit and the letter of the ADA.

Defining Disability. An important shift in the definition of disability has begun, and the hope for improved access is based on it. In the past, disability was defined almost exclusively from a medical perspective that focused on functional impairment. Disability was considered a defect in the individual, and the primary emphasis was on the cause of organic conditions. From this perspective, efforts to improve the functional capabilities of individuals were regarded as the only solution for disability. The resulting preoccupation with diagnosis fragmented the disability community by stressing the functional traits that divided them rather than the external obstacles that they faced as a common problem (Hahn, 1985).

Legislative decisions shifted the viewpoint to an economic one that concentrated on vocational limitations. This approach defined disability as a health-related limitation on the amount or kind of work that a person could perform. The economic definition has been widely adopted in income maintenance and support programs that equate disability with unemployability or that define it as an inability to engage in substantial gainful activity. By focusing on the capacity to work at the expense of other life activities, this approach is not only unidimensional, but it also makes some questionable assumptions about the connection between impairment and productivity, assumptions that advances in assistive technology are challenging (Hahn, 1985).

Legislation and rules adopted in the 1970s encouraged the development of a sociopolitical or interactional approach that defined disability as a product of the interaction between the individual and the environment. Whereas both of the earlier definitions regarded disability primarily as a personal limitation, the interactional view stresses the critical role of the environment in determining the meaning of disability (Hahn, 1985).

Recommendation: Disability cannot be defined simply by functional capabilities or occupational skills. A comprehensive understanding of disability requires us to examine the architectural, institutional, informational, and attitudinal environments that disabled people encounter. Higher education must examine its disability-related services, policies, practices, and activities to ensure that it incorporates this new definition into the institutional culture.

Organizing and Structuring Services. Higher education's primary response to the barriers that disabled students encounter has been to accommodate the physical, sensory, and cognitive impairments of individuals, not to make permanent changes in the academic environment with which students must cope. The existing modifications and adjustments have been made by a variety of units, including physical plant, parking, transportation, libraries, academic assistance centers, recreational sports, and computer services. Some of these units are tightly coupled with the disability service office, and some are not. Generally, the ways in which disability-related services have been organized do not make administrative roles and lines of authority clear. As a result, communication has been inconsistent. Service fragmentation, poor quality control, and questionable access are other consequences (Fairweather and Albert, 1991).

The terms *individualized* and *flexible* often hide the fact that services and accommodations are developed and provided as if they were a privilege, not a right. Too often, such an approach grants permission to continue business as usual, as if institutions did not need to change their systems and procedures in ways that eliminated the constant need to request and arrange accommodations.

Recommendation: To enhance communication, provide reliable access, and modify environments, higher education must work to centralize and standardize its disability access efforts. A single office should coordinate reasonable accommodations and disability-related services. And while the institution continues to provide individualized service to students with disabilities, it should increase the emphasis placed on designing and modifying environments permanently. Some people find it difficult to imagine an environment that has been adapted to the needs of everyone, including people with a variety of disabilities, but higher education is a prime environment for demonstrations of new technology and restructured systems and habitats.

The competing medical and interactional models that evolved in research on disability see different solutions to the problems of the disabled population: The medical model emphasizes service delivery. The interactional model highlights the rights of people with disabilities. These differences seem to reflect contrasting estimates of the potential for environmental change: The functional limitation perspective views the provision of extensive services as the most appropriate way of assisting disabled persons in surroundings that cannot or will not be adapted to their needs and desires. Proponents of the minority group orientation refuse to give up a vision of a world that treats these modifications as a right, not as a privilege or special concession. Obviously, until the structural alterations have been made, a broad range of social services must be provided. Yet the vision of a society in which environmental adaptations are viewed as aspects of the nation's basic commitment to freedom and equality must not be sacrificed. Programs and policies that regard the delivery of services as the sole, exclusive, or principal means of aiding disabled individuals may ultimately prove to be incomplete and even self-defeating (Hahn, 1987).

Defining Access. Access to higher education means much more than being able to get into a building, move around in it, use the rest rooms and drinking fountains, and park close by or use the transit service. Creating barrier-free environments means attending not only to grounds and buildings but also to attitudes and information as well.

Attitudinal Access. Attitudes are a key ingredient in the success or failure of students with disabilities in postsecondary education. The attitudes not only of disabled students but of nondisabled students, faculty, administrators, and student services personnel have profound effects on the integration of students with disabilities into the academic community.

Student affairs professionals need to provide training, consultation, and outreach to other members of the campus community in order to ensure access for students with disabilities. Many disability service offices are seeing increased requests for training, doubtless as a result of the ADA, especially on hidden disabilities, such as psychiatric and learning disabilities.

Recommendation: In order to ensure equal opportunity for disabled students, the institution must be ready to advocate, develop, and model disability access. Researchers argue that the best means to increase understanding, reduce prejudice, enhance comfort, and facilitate interaction between nondisabled and disabled individuals is to enforce laws and provide education, training, and extended close contact on an equal basis. Such activities as role plays in which nondisabled students simulate being blind, deaf, or wheelchair users have been shown to be ineffective, and they may even reinforce existing negative stereotypes about people with disabilities. However, types of role play with a problem-solving component could be effective, and they should be explored further in the college context (Fichten, 1988).

Access to Information and Technology. Access to information and technology is one major component of efforts to create barrier-free environments. Access to information can be defined as all tasks related to listening, speaking, reading, and writing as well as access to information tools, such as computers and telephones. Experience tells us that blind, deaf, and some learning-disabled students often face discrimination because the institution refuses to switch from standard methods of communicating to new methods that include people with disabilities. There is little excuse for unwillingness to accommodate people who cannot see or hear or who may not understand what they can see or hear.

Recommendation: For all information tasks, there is modern technology that can assist people with disabilities. The challenge for higher education is to create mechanisms that provide and support such technology. The ADA obligates public institutions to remove communication barriers whenever and wherever possible. It requires them to supply auxiliary aids and services in order to ensure access to information. These aids and services include sign language interpreters; assistive listening devices; TDDs; open and closed captioning; readers; taped texts; materials in alternate print formats, such as braille, large print, and electronic media; and adapted computers.

Physical Access. The signals regarding accessibility to grounds and facilities continue to be mixed. New construction and renovations are completed that pay little attention to functionality or to the actual users of the resulting environment. The six-foot, nondisabled, young male still seems to be the standard for architectural design.

The ADA guidelines themselves set forth different standards for existing facilities, new construction, and alterations. Jarrow (1992) notes that existing facilities must remove architectural, communication, and transportation barriers where readily achievable. Readily achievable is defined as "easily accomplishable" and as being able to be carried out without much difficulty or expense. For new construction, the standards for full accessibility are to be followed, regardless of the cost of implementation. When facilities are altered or renovated in any major way, the altered area must be made readily accessible to and usable by people with disabilities to the maximum extent feasible. If colleges and universities operate a transportation service for nondisabled people, transportation must also be available to disabled individuals such that, "when viewed in its entirety," the level of service provided is equivalent to the level of service available to others. The ADA says also that institutions need to develop emergency and evacuation policies regarding various institutional settings and facilities.

Recommendation: We must make facilities and sites work for everyone, not just for a generic physical standard that really does not exist. We must go beyond minima to optima and institutionalize the concept of universal design by designing buildings, systems, procedures, and activities that everyone can use. For example, automatic door openers are helpful for delivery people and children in strollers as well as for people who use wheelchairs. We must stop thinking "special," because the consequence of "special" is "separate."

Funding Accommodations and Services. The standard question, Who pays? applies to disability services in higher education. In some states, the institution pays. In other states, the Division of Rehabilitation Services (DRS) pays for some or all accommodations. For years, it has been recognized that many elementary and secondary school students have needs for which the state must provide special funding. However, although Section 504 of the Rehabilitation Act of 1973 and the ADA both require states to develop policies in this area, most states are no farther along than they were twenty years ago in funding disabled student services in postsecondary institutions.

Current institutional funding remains problematic in several ways: Salaries and other operating expenses for disability services differ among institutions, as do their mission, function, and the academic preparation and needs of their disabled students. Programs serving small numbers of students have higher costs than larger programs because they cannot take advantage of economies of scale. The cost of serving disabled students varies with their disabilities. Some disabled students require high-cost services, such as interpreters. Others may only need low-cost services, such as information and referral. The true costs of funding adequate services for disabled students are difficult to establish. The current costs reflect only the funds available for current services and bear little relationship to real needs (professionally trained staff on every campus, substantial outreach efforts, involvement by disabled students in cocurricular activities, reliance on volunteers for reasonable accommodations that are reliable and effective (California Postsecondary Education Commission, 1986).

Recommendation: The United States needs to address the issue of funding for students in higher education with disabilities. It is clear that colleges and universities will continue to bear an increased financial responsibility for the provision of services and environmental modifications. Institutions must not only lobby their state and federal legislators but also decide where disability access fits within their own campus or system. In spite of tight funding, access for disabled students cannot be looked upon as a "would be nice"agenda item. Campuses need consistent, adequate, and annually recurring funding (Bonney, 1988).

Evaluating Services. Intensified interest in disabled college students has intensified interest in disability services. External pressure for accountability and the institution's own need to determine the effectiveness of current services require the institution to improve its evaluation of disability services. How effective are the services at ensuring equitable access for students with disabilities? Have disability services become counterproductive? How can we assure that disability services do not become counterproductive?

While many view disability service offices as tremendously effective and successful, this perception is rarely based on an internal or external validation of effectiveness or success. Many student affairs professionals lack expertise in evaluation research (the systematic collection of information) and evaluation (the use of research results in decision making). As a result, their efforts to determine effectiveness have been sporadic and unsatisfying.

Recommendation: Both process evaluation (program monitoring) and outcome or impact evaluation (measurement of a program's short- and long-term effects) are important management tools. Evaluations should be conducted to meet external demands, improve services, improve efficiency, increase staff morale, cut costs, increase unit credibility, and increase coordination and communication.

Collaborating with Faculty. Postsecondary institutions have not clarified the rights and responsibilities of individual faculty members regarding course accommodations for disabled students. The procedures that many institutions have implemented require students to identify their disability to the disability service office, which is responsible for documenting the disability and determining reasonable accommodations. Students then may be instructed to contact their professors and request the accommodations that have already been decided on. Reportedly, faculty members have indicated their displeasure with such procedures by challenging either the disability service office assessment of disability or the need for accommodation; by refusing to help students arrange accommodations; and by demanding to review the documentary evidence of the student's disability. The result of such hostile responses from faculty members is that disabled students are denied effective accommodation. The problem is compounded when the procedures in place at the institution fail to identify an individual or group responsible for addressing and resolving disagreements between individual faculty members and the disability service office. The student is trapped between them (Heyward, Lawton, and Associates, 1991).

Recommendation: Policies on course modification must address questions of faculty participation directly. These policies should convey to faculty members that they do not have the right to contest the existence of disabilities that have been properly documented and that they do not have the right to refuse to provide necessary accommodations. Faculty should be given an opportunity to participate in decision making regarding the type and range of accommodations that will be provided for classroom instruction. The message should be that accommodations *must* be provided for properly documented disabilities but all parties—students, representatives of the disability service office, and faculty members—should work together to fashion effective accommodations that give students meaningful access while maintaining the academic integrity of the instructional program. Finally, these policies should establish mechanisms for resolving disagreements between disability service staff, students, and individual faculty members (Heyward, Lawton, and Associates, 1991).

Conclusion

It is almost two decades since the passage of Section 504, and people with disabilities are still experiencing less of almost everything in life—less money, less employment, less social life, and less education. According to a national survey by Louis Harris and Associates (1986), only 60 percent of the adults with disabilities in the United States finish high school, compared to 85 percent of nondisabled students; and only 29 percent of those with disabilities have attended at least some college, compared to 48 percent of nondisabled students, and the college-going rate for disabled students is about half that of nondisabled students.

The Americans with Disabilities Act (ADA) has been hailed as civil rights legislation for people with disabilities. The ADA has heightened awareness within the disability community, and early responses from students indicate that they identify more closely with this legislation than with Section 504. This is likely to mean that demand for services will increase, as will attention to the areas in which colleges and universities are out of compliance with Section 504. The ADA also has extensive implications for employment, and these implications will certainly have an impact on the potential for employment of disabled students after enrollment. Higher education must continue to respond. The new political agenda of the disability community will not allow higher education to keep the topic out of sight and thereby out of mind. Institutions must be proactive and incorporate the interactional perspective on disability into their services, facilities, activities, and programs. Educational programs must inspire, not merely reflect, the world's values.

References

Bonney, S. Testimony presented on behalf of the Association on Handicapped Student Service Programs in Postsecondary Education (AHSSPPE) to the National Council on the

Handicapped, July 23, 1987. In *Capitalizing on the Future, Proceedings of the 1987 AHSSPPE Conference.* Columbus, Ohio: AHSSPPE, 1988.

California Postsecondary Education Commission. *Expanding Educational Opportunities for Students with Disabilities.* Sacramento, Calif.: California Postsecondary Education Commission, 1986.

Fairweather, J., and Albert, J. "Organizational and Administrative Implications for Serving College Students with Disabilities." In H. Cheatham and others (eds.), *Cultural Pluralism on Campus.* Alexandria, Va.: ACPA Media Board Publications, 1991.

Fichten, C. "Students with Disabilities in Higher Education: Attitudes and Beliefs That Affect Integration." In H. Yuker (ed.), *Attitudes Toward Persons with Disabilities.* New York: Springer, 1988.

Hahn, H. "Toward a Politics of Disability: Definitions, Disciplines, and Policies." *Social Science Journal,* 1985, 22(4), 87–105.

Hahn, H. "Civil Rights for Disabled Americans: The Foundation of a Political Agenda." In A. Gartner and T. Joe (eds.), *Images of Disabled, Disabling Images.* New York: Praeger, 1987.

Harris, L., and Associates. *The ICD Survey of Disabled Americans.* New York: Louis Harris and Associates, 1986.

Heyward, S., Lawton, D., and Associates. "Provision of Academic Accommodations." *Disability Accommodations Digest,* 1991, 1(1),1–4.

Jarrow, J. *The ADA's Impact on Postsecondary Education.* Columbus, Ohio: Association of Higher Education and Disability, 1992.

U.S. Department of Education. *Access for Handicapped Students to Higher Education: A Reference Handbook.* Washington, D.C.: U.S. Dept. of Education, 1981.

SUE KROEGER *is director of disability services at the University of Minnesota–Twin Cities.*

JUDY SCHUCK *is associate dean of student services and former director of the office for students with disabilities at Minneapolis Community College, Minneapolis, Minnesota.*

*This chapter provides an annotated list of resources for student
services and disability personnel.*

Resource Guide: A Compendium
of Literature and Organizations

Judy Schuck, Sue Kroeger

With the increase in disability services in higher education over the past ten
years and the recent passage of the Americans with Disabilities Act (ADA),
information and organizations directly or indirectly related to postsecondary
education and students with disabilities have proliferated. This chapter is
divided into two sections: literature and organizations.

Literature

The entries in this section have been selected from a variety of sources. They
address topics ranging from accessible professional conferences to faculty in-
service and legal assistance. Resources that address issues surrounding the ADA
have been emphasized. The annotations aim to help readers determine
whether a reference will be useful for their concern or question. The authors
acknowledge the information and assistance received from Rhona Hartman
and the HEATH Resource Center in preparation of this chapter.

ABLEDATA

    A computerized listing of commercially available adaptive devices that aid
in rehabilitation and independent living for all types of disabilities, ABLEDATA
is available through the National Rehabilitation Information Center (NARIC),
8455 Colesville Road, Suite 935, Silver Spring, MD 20910, (301) 588–9284
(V/TTY) or (800) 346–2742 (V/TTY).

American Association of Community Colleges. *ADA: Audit, Transition Plan, and
Policy Statement for Higher Education.* Washington, D.C.: American Association
of Community Colleges, 1993.

The American Association of Community Colleges (AACC) developed this two-part publication to help community colleges comply with the ADA. Focused on how to accommodate students with disabilities in both academic and student affairs, it contains an extensive checklist of resources to assist administrators. It can be ordered from AACC Publications, P.O. Box 1737, Salisbury, MD 21802, (410) 546–0391.

Aune, E., Johnson, D., Bagget. D., Aase, S., Carlson, S., and Kroeger, S. *Career Development and Employment for College Students with Disabilities: An Annotated Bibliography*. Minneapolis: Disability Services, University of Minnesota, 1992.
This bibliography was prepared by the University of Minnesota and the University of Massachusetts with support from the U.S. Department of Education's Office of Special Education and Rehabilitation Services. Forty-one articles published since 1987 are abstracted. Topic areas include career development; employment; and trends, attitudes, and guidelines.

Barnett, Lynn (ed.). *Directory of Disability Support Services in Community Colleges*. Washington, D.C.: American Association of Community Colleges, 1992.
This directory provides prospective students and their advisers with information about trends in community college enrollment among students with disabilities and about special services provided by specific colleges. Single copies are available free of charge from the HEATH Resource Center.

Brinckerhoff, L. *College Students with Learning Disabilities*. Columbus, Ohio: AHEAD, 1992.
This inexpensive brochure, a general information piece originally produced by the McBurney Resource Center at the University of Wisconsin, Madison, is an excellent resource for widespread distribution to faculty and students.

Brown, Carl (ed.). *Computer Access in Higher Education for Students with Disabilities*. Cupertino: California Community Colleges High Tech Center Training Unit, 1986.
This manual gives a comprehensive overview of assistive computer technology. It includes criteria for the selection of hardware and software.

Dahlke, Connie. *Support Programs in Higher Education for Students with Disabilities: Access to All*. Gaithersburg, Md.: Aspen Publishers, 1991.
This manual provides information on college students with disabilities and reasonable accommodations.

Disability Accommodation Digest. AHEAD, Columbus, Ohio.
Edited by Salome Heyward, this newsletter addresses legal issues surrounding Section 504 and the ADA. Relevant court cases and Office of Civil Rights findings are summarized, and a regular column answers readers' questions. To subscribe, contact AHEAD, P.O. Box 21192, Columbus, OH 43221–0192.

The Disability Rag. Avocado Press, 1962 Roanoke, Louisville, KY 40205.
This bimonthly magazine covers the disability rights movement.

Duston, R. L. *What Every College and University Administrator Needs to Know About the ADA and Why.* Washington, D.C.: Schmeltzer, Aptaker, & Shepard, 1991.
This overview of the ADA's requirements is intended to help college and university administrators comply with the law. It is available from the publisher, Schmeltzer, Aptaker, & Shepard, Counselors at Law, 2600 Virginia Avenue N.W., Suite 1000, Washington, DC 20037, (202) 333-3434.

Financial Aid for Students with Disabilities—1992. Washington, D.C.: HEATH Resource Center, American Council on Education, 1992.
This brochure, which reflects new provisions of the Higher Education Reauthorization Act, lists a number of new disability-specific scholarships, identifies selected new financial aid publications, and explains in plain English how to access the regular financial aid system. Single copies are available free of charge from HEATH.

Foreign Language Learning and Learning Disabilities Conference Information Packets. Washington, D.C.: American University, 1992.
These packets, which include handouts and articles from the conference, are helpful to anyone dealing with the issues of second language waivers and substitutions. Packets are available from the English Language Institute, McKinley 206, The American University, 4400 Massachusetts Avenue N.W., Washington, DC 20016-8031.

HEATH Resource Directory. Washington, D.C.: HEATH Resource Center, American Council on Education, 1992.
This directory, designed for persons with disabilities, families, counselors, teachers, administrators, and others, highlights some useful resources in the major areas of interest in the field; it is not a comprehensive listing.

Henderson, C. *College Freshmen with Disabilities: A Statistical Profile.* Washington, D.C.: HEATH Resource Center, American Council on Education, 1992.
This publication reports on the 140,000 students with disabilities who were first-time freshmen in more than 3,000 institutions of higher education in 1991.

Jarrow, J. E. *Subpart E: The Impact of Section 504 on Postsecondary Education.* Columbus, Ohio: AHEAD, 1992.
This booklet is a detailed reference regarding the support and services mandated for students with disabilities under Section 504. It reviews relevant findings from the courts and the Office for Civil Rights and answers the questions most often asked about interpretation of Section 504.

Jarrow, J. E. *Title by Title: The ADA's Impact on Postsecondary Education.* Columbus, Ohio: AHEAD, 1992.

This reference book reviews the ADA title by title with specific reference to postsecondary education and explains the relationship between Section 504 and the ADA.

Jarrow, J. E., and Park, C. B. *Accessible Meetings and Conventions.* Columbus, Ohio: AHEAD, 1992.

This resource provides organizational and meeting facility planners with basic information on compliance with the ADA.

Johnson, D., Aune, E., and Aase, S. *Putting Ability to Work: Career Development and Disability.* Minneapolis: Disability Services, University of Minnesota, 1992.

This manual, development of which was supported by grants to the University of Minnesota from the Office of Special Education and Rehabilitation Services, U.S. Department of Education, is designed for training campus professionals, community employers, mentors, and mentees. The manual covers legislation, etiquette and disclosure, disability categories, case studies, career exploration and decision making, job seeking and job analysis, and resources, and it contains scripts, handouts, and overheads.

Johnson, M. E. (ed.). *People with Disabilities Explain It All for You: Your Guide to the Public Accommodations Requirements of the ADA.* Louisville, Ky.: Avocado Press, 1992.

This book, written by consumers, is a humorous, jargon-free, but thorough and accurate explanation of regulations in the ADA relating to public accommodations.

King, W., and Jarrow, J. E. *Testing Accommodations for Students with Disabilities.* Columbus, Ohio: AHEAD, 1990.

This guide is written for the service provider in higher education who is responsible for arranging testing accommodations for students with disabilities. Clear philosophical guidelines for operating a test accommodations program are outlined. Process is discussed in detail, and sample forms are included.

King, W., and Jarrow, J. E. *Testing Accommodations for Persons with Disabilities: A Guide for Licensure, Certification, and Credentialing.* Columbus, Ohio: AHEAD, 1992.

This guide was funded by the U.S. Department of Justice to provide general information about ADA provisions referring to agencies, institutions, and organizations that provide examinations leading to licensure, certification, or credentialing for secondary and postsecondary education, professional, and trade purposes.

Kroeger, S., and Pazandak, C. "Women with Disabilities and the College Experience: Report of a Study." Paper read at the American Psychological Association meeting, Boston, August 1990.

This paper reports on a study conducted in 1990 to assess the attitudes and experiences of students with disabilities who dropped out or graduated from the University of Minnesota. This study is set in the context of data from multiple sources, which show that women are at an educational, occupational, and economic disadvantage when compared with men and that women with disabilities are the most seriously disadvantaged.

Mangrum, C. T., II, and Strichart, S. S. *College and the Learning-Disabled Student.* Philadelphia: Grune & Stratton, 1988.

A comprehensive and practical resource for anyone interested in services for learning-disabled (LD) college students, this book reviews the development of these services, the characteristics of LD students, important program components, and teaching techniques. Charts, sample forms, and lists of resources are included.

The Mouth. Free Hand Press, Rochester, N.Y.

This bimonthly magazine covers the disability rights movement. For information, write to Free Hand Press, 61 Brighton Street, Rochester NY 14607.

Office of Special Education and Rehabilitative Services (OSERS), U.S. Department of Education. *Summary of Existing Legislation Affecting People with Disabilities.* Washington, D.C.: U.S. Government Printing Office, 1991.

This 235-page paperback summary is a useful reference for anyone who writes proposals, presents conferences or workshops, conducts research on disability issues, or advocates for individuals with disabilities. It is available from the Clearinghouse on Disability Information, OSERS, Room 3132 Switzer Building, Washington, DC 20202–2524, (202) 205–8241.

Postsecondary LD Network News. Postsecondary Learning Disability Unit, A. J. Pappanikou Center on Special Education and Rehabilitation, University of Connecticut, Storrs.

This newsletter, which is published three times a year and distributed to more than five hundred subscribers in the United States and Canada, was originally designed to meet the needs of postsecondary service providers who work with learning-disabled (LD) college students. Its scope has expanded to include information relevant to all LD adults and a wide range of service providers. The newsletter can be ordered from the University of Connecticut, Pappanikou Center on Special Education and Rehabilitation, U-64, 249 Glenbrook Road, Storrs, CT 06269–2064.

Reading and Learning Disabilities: A Resource Guide. Washington, D.C.: National Information Center for Children and Youth with Disabilities, 1992.

This twelve-page briefing paper by the National Information Center for Children and Youth with Disabilities (NICHCY) includes information on how an adult can determine whether a learning disability is present, types of agencies where an adult can be tested, questions to ask evaluators, an extensive bibliography, and a listing of national clearinghouses and federal and state agencies that can provide additional information. A single copy is available free from NICHCY, P.O. Box 1492, Washington, DC 20013, (800) 999–5599.

Scheiber, B., and Talpers, J. *Unlocking Potential: College and Other Choices for Learning Disabled People—A Step-by-Step Guide.* Bethesda, Md.: Adler and Adler, 1987.

This transition resource for service providers and consumers focuses on the selection of appropriate college, technical school, or other postsecondary programs; the admissions process; coursework accommodations; support services; the use of new technology; and personal adjustment.

Schuck, J. "Teaching with Compassion: A Lifeline for Students with Learning Disabilities." *Faculty Development*, 1992, 5(2), 1–3.

This brief article on LD students in higher education, which is designed for faculty in-service training, addresses such topics as characteristics and teaching strategies. It is available through the Bush Regional Collaboration in Faculty Development, Galtier Plaza, Suite 401, Box 40, 175 Fifth Street E., St. Paul, MN 55101–2901.

Shaw, S. F., and Shaw, S. R. "LD College Programming: A Bibliography." *Support Services for LD Students in Postsecondary Education: A Compendium of Readings*, 1987, 2, 117–127.

This bibliography of more than 160 references includes information on transition, characteristics, diagnosis, social skills, vocational preparation, program effectiveness, and program evaluation.

Spiers, E. (ed.). *Transition Resource Guide.* Washington, D.C.: HEATH Resource Center, American Council on Education, 1992.

This guide includes articles, lists of contacts and resources, and selected materials developed about and for students with disabilities who are leaving high school and beginning some sort of postsecondary education or training. Single free copies are available from HEATH.

Vogel, S. *College Students with Learning Disabilities: A Handbook.* Pittsburgh, Pa.: Learning Disabilities Association, 1993.

This forty-five-page handbook is designed to be used by students with learning disabilities, admissions officers, faculty and staff, and administrators. In addition to helpful information for students and faculty, it contains a list of ways in which administrators can help to improve campuswide services for students with learning disabilities and a list of recommendations for graduate and professional schools.

Organizations

The public and private organizations listed in this section offer information and activities related to adults with disabilities, particularly in reference to the involvement of adults with disabilities in higher education. These organizations provide assistance, much of it free of charge, through publications, toll-free information lines, and professional development activities.

ADA Technical Assistance Centers, (800) 949–4232.
    Ten regional centers provide assistance on all titles of the ADA. On dialing the toll-free number, the caller is automatically connected to a consultant in his or her own region.

Architectural and Transportation Barriers Compliance Board, 1111 18th Street N.W., Suite 501, Washington, DC 20036–3894, (800) 872–2253.
    The board processes complaints about inaccessibility in federal facilities and provides technical assistance in accessible design and barrier removal in architecture, transportation, and communication.

Association on Higher Education and Disability (AHEAD), P.O. Box 21192, Columbus, OH 43221, (614) 488–4972 (V/TT).
    The Association on Higher Education and Disability (AHEAD)—the former Association on Handicapped Student Service Programs in Postsecondary Education (AHSSPPE)—is a national nonprofit professional organization with members from more than six hundred institutions of higher education. Technical assistance, annual conferences, timely publications, and membership in special-interest groups related to specific disability groups are available from AHEAD.

California Community Colleges High Tech Center Training Unit, 21050 McClellan Road, Cupertino, CA 95014, (408) 996–4636.
    The California Community Colleges High Tech Center Training Unit provides a wide variety of training opportunities, telephone support, site visits, and advanced levels of technical support for hardware and software operation primarily to California community colleges, but its services are also available on a fee basis to a limited number of professionals outside the state. Chapter Eight in this volume reviews the work of the High Tech Centers.

Closing the Gap (CTG), P.O. Box 68, Henderson, MN 56044, (612) 248–3294.
    CTG publishes a bimonthly newspaper, hosts an annual national conference on assistive computer applications, and offers hands-on training to special education and rehabilitation professionals.

Disability Rights Education and Defense Fund, Inc. (DREDF), 2212 Sixth Street, Berkeley, CA 94710, (510) 644–2555 (V/TTY) or (800) 466–4232.

The Disability Rights Education and Defense Fund, a national disability rights law and policy center, offers publications; training programs on disability civil rights issues, legal support and advocacy, and policy analysis; and referral to local sources of help.

HEATH Resource Center, One Dupont Circle, Suite 800, Washington, DC 20036–1193, (202) 939–9320 (V/TDD) or (800) 544–3284 (V/TDD).

The HEATH Resource Center operates the National Clearinghouse on Postsecondary Education for Handicapped Individuals. Its mandate is to provide information about the increasing variety of postsecondary options available to people with disabilities. Chapter Three in this volume reviews some of the model transition programs that the HEATH Resource Center can provide information about.

IBM National Support Center for People with Disabilities, P.O. Box 2150, Atlanta, GA 30055, (800) 426–4832.

The IBM National Support Center for People with Disabilities provides information on computerized systems and technology for people with disabilities in the workplace, home, and school environments. Resource guides and instructional videotapes are available.

Learning Disabilities Association (LDA), 4156 Library Road, Pittsburgh, PA 15234, (412) 341–1515.

The Learning Disabilities Association (LDA)—the former Association for Children and Adults with Learning Disabilities—is a national organization of professionals and consumers devoted to defining and finding solutions for the broad spectrum of learning problems. Services include a resource center of publications, a bimonthly newsletter, and referral to local LDA chapters.

Mainstream, Inc., 3 Bethesda Metro Center, Suite 830, Bethesda, MD 20814, (301) 654–2400 (V/TDD).

Mainstream, Inc., works with employers and service providers to increase employment opportunities for people with disabilities. Publications and training on all relevant disability employment issues and regional directories of organizations that provide technical assistance on compliance with the ADA are available.

National Center on Youth and Disability (NCYD), University of Minnesota, Harvard Street at East River Road, Minneapolis, MN 55455, (612) 626–2825 or (800) 333–6293.

The National Center on Youth and Disability offers a national resource library with a computerized, comprehensive data base containing information about youth with chronic illnesses. It publishes CYDLINE Reviews, a series of bibliographies that include annotated listings of bibliographic, training, and educational materials and programs.

National Science Foundation Program for Persons with Disabilities (PPD), Room 1225, 1800 G Street N.W., Washington, DC 20550, (202) 357–7461.

The National Science Foundation Program for Persons with Disabilities promotes full inclusion and participation of people with disabilities in academic studies leading to careers in science and engineering.

Office of Civil Rights (OCR), U.S. Department of Education, Suite 5000, 330 C Street S.W., Washington, DC 20202–1100, (202) 205–5413 or (202) 205–9683 (TTY).

The Office of Civil Rights maintains ten regional offices to answer questions on matters of legal interpretation regarding higher education and Section 504 and the ADA.

Orton Dyslexia Society, Chester Building, Suite 382, 8600 LaSalle Road, Baltimore, MD 21286–2044, (410) 296–0232 or (800) 222–3123.

The Orton Dyslexia Society is an international scientific and educational association for consumers and professionals concerned specifically with dyslexia. Publications and local chapters in many states are available.

PACER Center, Inc., 4826 Chicago Avenue S., Minneapolis, MN 55417–1055, (612) 827–2966 (V/TDD).

PACER—Parent Advocacy Coalition for Educational Rights—is a consumer group that offers training, advocacy, and a newsletter for youth with disabilities and their families.

President's Committee on Employment of People with Disabilities, 1331 F Street N.W., Suite 300, Washington, DC 20004–1107, (202) 376–6200 or (202) 376–6205 (TDD).

The President's Committee on Employment of People with Disabilities is a national source of information and assistance concerning employment and people with disabilities. It can refer callers to committees at state and local levels. Information regarding timelines and implementation for the ADA is also available.

Recordings for the Blind (RFB), 20 Roszel Road, Princeton, NJ 08540, (609) 452–0606 or (800) 221–4792.

Recordings for the Blind (RFB), which tapes educational books for people with visual or learning disabilities, will record textbooks not in its master library at the request of blind or print-disabled students. There is a one-time application fee. Equipment for use with RFB recordings can be obtained through the Library of Congress.

Society for Disability Studies (SDS), c/o Sharon Barnartt, Gallaudet University, 8th and Florida N.E., Washington, DC 20002, (202) 651–5160.

The Society for Disability Studies is a nonprofit scientific and educational organization that promotes interdisciplinary research on humanistic and social scientific aspects of disability and chronic illness.

Trace Research and Development Center. Waisman Center, 1500 Highland Avenue, Madison, WI 53705, (608) 262–6966 or (608) 263–5408 (TDD).

The Trace Research and Development Center has a wealth of information on the communication and other needs of severely disabled individuals that current microcomputer technology may not be able to meet. Its work helps individuals access postsecondary training programs by meeting communication needs and developing alternate methods of accessing computers.

JUDY SCHUCK is associate dean of student services and former director of the office for students with disabilities at Minneapolis Community College, Minneapolis, Minnesota.

SUE KROEGER is director of disability services at the University of Minnesota–Twin Cities.

INDEX

Aase, S., 55, 112, 114
ABLEDATA, 111
Academic skill building, for learning disabled, 75
Access: attitudinal, 105–106; to information and technology, 106; of learning disabled, 74–75; physical, 106–107; programmatic, 12–14; recommendations on, 105–107; right to meaningful, 18–20; Section 504 mandate on, 10
Accommodation: case law and legislation on, 14–15; definition of, 8, 63; effective, 24–27; for learning disabled, 74–75; as program element, 63. *See also* Auxiliary aids
ADA Technical Assistance Centers, 117
Adelphi University, 35
Administrators, and transition services, 39–40
Admission(s): assessing qualified status for, 23–24; of learning disabled, 73–74; Section 504 mandates on, 10; and transition services, 40–41
Advocacy, as program element, 64–65. See also Self-advocacy training
African Americans: cultural differences of, 81–84; and special education, 80–81
Albert, J., 52, 66, 105
Alexander v. Choate, 18, 19, 21
Allegra, R., 3
Aloia, G. F., 81
Aloia, S. D., 81
American Association of Collegiate Registrars and Admissions Officers (AACRAO), 74
American Association of Community Colleges, 111
American Council on Education, 9
Americans with Disabilities Act (ADA), 15–16, 17, 33, 59, 60, 61, 65; and future for disabled, 103, 109; literature on, 111–117; organizations for information on, 117–121; recommendations on issues with, 104–109; on technology, 89
Americans Disabled for Accessible Public Transportation v. Skinner, 20
Ammirati, T., 62
Anderson v. University of Wisconsin, 20

Anderson, W. R., 34
Architectural barriers, 12–13
Architectural and Transportation Barriers Compliance Board, 117
Arizona State University, 35
Arizona, University of, 65
Arline v. School Board of Nassau County, 21, 22
Asian Americans, 82, 83, 84
Assessment: individualized, 21–24; of learning disabled, 71–73; as program element, 61–62. *See also* Testing
Assistive computer technologies, 92–93; for blindness, 93–94; for deafness and aural impairment, 97; future of, 100–102; for learning disabilities, 96–97; for low vision, 94–95; for orthopedic disabilities, 95–96. *See also* High Tech Centers
Association on Handicapped Student Service Programs in Postsecondary Education (AHSSPPE), 34
Association on Higher Education and Disability (AHEAD), 34, 117–118
Astin, A. W., 45, 47, 49
Attitudinal barriers, 12
Aune, E., 47, 112, 114
Aural impairment: assistive computer technologies with, 97; ruling on access with, 14
Auxiliary aids: ruling on financial responsibility for, 26–27; Section 504 mandates on, 10–11

Bagget, D., 112
Ball State University, 35
Ball-Brown, B., 3, 79, 88
Banning, J. H., 47
Barnett, L., 112
Beal, P. E., 48
Block, L. S., 2–3, 69, 78
Bloom, A., 46
Bonney, S., 60, 108
Brennan v. Stewart, 22
Brinckerhoff, L., 75, 112
Brown v. Washington University, 15
Brown, C., 3, 89, 102, 112
Brown, R. D., 56
Bush, G., 15

121

ORDERING INFORMATION

NEW DIRECTIONS FOR STUDENT SERVICES is a series of paperback books that offers guidelines and programs for aiding students in their total development—emotional, social, and physical, as well as intellectual. Books in the series are published quarterly in spring, summer, fall, and winter and are available for purchase by subscription as well as by single copy.

SUBSCRIPTIONS for 1993 cost $47.00 for individuals (a savings of 25 percent over single-copy prices) and $62.00 for institutions, agencies, and libraries. Please do not send institutional checks for personal subscriptions. Standing orders are accepted.

SINGLE COPIES cost $15.95 when payment accompanies order. (California, New Jersey, New York, and Washington, D.C., residents please include appropriate sales tax.) Billed orders will be charged postage and handling.

DISCOUNTS FOR QUANTITY ORDERS are available. Please write to the address below for information.

ALL ORDERS must include either the name of an individual or an official purchase order number. Please submit your order as follows:
    Subscriptions: specify series and year subscription is to begin
    Single copies: include individual title code (such as SS1)

MAIL ALL ORDERS TO:
    Jossey-Bass Publishers
    350 Sansome Street
    San Francisco, California 94104-1342

FOR SINGLE-COPY SALES OUTSIDE OF THE UNITED STATES, CONTACT:
    Maxwell Macmillan International Publishing Group
    866 Third Avenue
    New York, New York 10022-6221

FOR SUBSCRIPTION SALES OUTSIDE OF THE UNITED STATES, CONTACT:
    any international subscription agency or Jossey-Bass directly.

OTHER TITLES AVAILABLE IN THE
NEW DIRECTIONS FOR STUDENT SERVICES SERIES
Margaret J. Barr, Editor-in-Chief
M. Lee Upcraft, Associate Editor